REVOLUTION AND REPETITION

ABOUT
QUANTUM
BOOKS

QUANTUM, THE UNIT OF
EMITTED ENERGY. A QUANTUM
BOOK IS A SHORT STUDY
DISTINCTIVE FOR THE AUTHOR'S
ABILITY TO OFFER A RICHNESS OF
DETAIL AND INSIGHT WITHIN
ABOUT ONE HUNDRED PAGES
OF PRINT. SHORT ENOUGH TO BE
READ IN AN EVENING AND
SIGNIFICANT ENOUGH
TO BE A BOOK

JEFFREY MEHLMAN

Revolution and Repetition

MARX / HUGO / BALZAC

UNIVERSITY OF CALIFORNIA PRESS
Berkeley Los Angeles London

79966

University of California Press
Berkeley and Los Angeles, California
University of California Press, Ltd.
London, England
Copyright © 1977 by
The Regents of the University of California
ISBN 0-520-03111-3
Library of Congress Catalog Card Number: 76-24589
Printed in the United States of America

For Alicia

Contents

Introduction

My effort in this book is to reopen, obliquely, through a series of readings, the question of the relation between Marx's writings and (the institution of) literature. It consists not in any attempted "application" of Marxian categories to literary texts, but in a delineation of how the phenomenon of revolution in France is refracted through two divergent series of writings. The first is comprised of works that Marx's best French readers, for understandable political reasons, have been unwilling to submit to any interpretative risks: *Class Struggles in France 1848–1850, The Eighteenth Brumaire of Louis Bonaparte,* and *The Civil War in France.* My hope is that these readings will be alive to that *linguistic—or textual—specificity* which, according to *The German Ideology,* is the bane of every idealist interpretation.[1] The second series moves through two exemplary nineteenth-century novels on revolution:

1. "We find that man also possesses 'consciousness' but, even so, not 'pure' consciousness. From the start the 'spirit' is afflicted with the curse of being 'burdened' with matter, which here makes its appearance in the form of agitated layers of air, sounds, in short, of language . . . . " *Die deutsche Ideologie* in Marx and Engels, Werke, III (Berlin: Dietz Verlag, 1969), p. 30.

Hugo's *Quatrevingt-treize* and Balzac's *Les Chouans.*
Whence the titles of the two chapters in this work, in
their deceptive simplicity: "History" and "Literature."

It may be wondered whether the intent of my argument is to superimpose that doublet—History/
Literature—on the terms comprising this book's title:
respectively "Revolution" and "Repetition." Ideally,
as the first chapter delineates the specific textuality of
Marx's writing, as the second moves toward the constitution of a certain historicity of the nineteenth-
century novel, and as they together intersect, chiasmatically, in a concluding footnote, the whole of my
analysis should comprise a demonstration of the *impossibility* of affirming that superimposition. For the
moment, however, emblematically, an elementary bit
of philology: the primary meaning of "revolution,"
our term for inaugural change, is astronomical—"the
action . . . of moving round in an orbit or circular
course; the return or recurrence of a point or period of
time" O.E.D.). To discover that repetition at the origin is not unrelated to the general project pursued in
these pages . . .

My distrust of "theories of reading" presented in
abstraction will become manifest in the second chapter. It may nevertheless be useful, in order to situate
my effort, to invoke a certain historicity of the act of
reading. For reasons I have elaborated elsewhere, but
which emerge intermittently in this essay, I regard the
strongest acts of reading currently available to us as
those comprised by the recent French interpretation of

Freud.[2] Consequently, although my analyses are by no means psychoanalytical in a conventional sense, both sections of this book are marked by an experience of Freud at his most provocative. The first may be regarded as a meditation on the perversity of the repetition compulsion in two of its most striking formulations: "the uncanny (*das Unheimliche*)" and the "death instinct."[3] The second engages at a crucial juncture that other limit-concept—or "bedrock"—of psychoanalysis: "castration." If this work is thus haunted by Freud, it is out of the conviction, however inconvenient, that *reading* today will tend to register its most radical effects by working in a calculated proximity to the French "tradition" of Freud.

This book is, then, an attempt to investigate what a certain twentieth century can learn from a series of nineteenth-century readings of the culminating sequence of the eighteenth. Increasingly, in the process, I found my discoveries engaging what seem to me the most important French interpretative projects of the last few years. Specifically, the reader will encounter in these pages Jean Laplanche's lectures on "anxiety" in

2. See my introduction to the anthology *French Freud* (*Yale French Studies*, 48, 1973) as well as *A Structural Study of Autobiography: Proust, Leiris, Sartre, Lévi-Strauss* (Ithaca: Cornell University Press, 1974) and the introduction to my translation of Jean Laplanche, *Life and Death in Psychoanalysis* (Baltimore: The Johns Hopkins University Press, 1976).

3. This section originally appeared in a French version, under the title "A partir du mot *unheimlich* chez Marx" in a special issue of *Critique*, 333 (February 1975), entitled "La psychanalyse vue du dehors."

Freud, Jacques Derrida's *Glas,* and, briefly but deci-
sively, in the course of a critique of Lukacs's "Balzac,"
Michel Foucault's genealogy of prisons, *Surveiller et
punir.* [4] Which is to say that at its most pedagogical this
volume will serve as a working introduction to what,
in all its diversity, may crudely be termed French
"post-structuralism."

Finally, a word of thanks: to my students at the
University of California, Berkeley, and at Johns Hopkins, who originally heard the matter of this book as a
course, and to Denis Hollier, in conversation with
whom, at Berkeley, many of these analyses were
spawned.

4. Laplanche, "Les normes morales et sociales, leur impact dans
la topique subjective" in *Bulletin de psychologie,* 306–307 (Paris,
1972–73); Derrida, *Glas* (Paris: Galilée, 1974); Foucault, *Surveiller et
punir: Naissance de la prison* (Paris: Gallimard, 1975).

I.

HISTORY

Disons que l'inconscient c'est le travailleur idéal, celui
dont Marx a fait la fleur de l'économie capitaliste dans
l'espoir de lui voir prendre le relais du discours du
maître; ce qui est arrivé en effet, bien que sous une
forme inattendue. Il y a des surprises en ces affaires de
discours, c'est même là le fait de l'inconscient.

— J. Lacan, Télévision

Along with a statute abolishing universal suffrage, the
Party of Order in France succeeded in 1850 in passing a
press law requiring every newspaper article to bear the
name of its author. Marx, in the fourth chapter of *Class
Struggles in France,* evokes the inhibiting effect that law
was to have on the circulation of news and emphasizes
the inability of the political reaction, at the time,
to tolerate the "sinister anonymity [*unheimliche
Anonymität*]" of *any* press, whatever its orientation (p.
101).[1] The cultural historian may be inclined to smile
upon encountering this most Freudian of terms within
Marx's text. That smile, moreover, will no doubt fade

---

1. References in the text to *Class Struggles in France 1848–1850* are
to the German edition: *Die Klassenkämpfe in Frankreich 1848 bis
1850* in *Werke,* VII (Berlin: Dietz Verlag, 1973). The translation,
occasionally modified, is that of International Publishers.

in the wake of its tenuous occasion, for the apparently coincidental repetition of the term designating "the uncanny" would seem by no means to threaten— to infiltrate—a certain exteriority in relation to psychoanalysis constituted by Marx's writings. Indeed, to the extent that a field of inquiry claiming to be *beyond* the concerns of psychoanalysis should be, in its written manifestations, commensurate with the text whose imperialistic incursions it would resist, Marx's writings, by dint of their deconstructive resources, would be among the very few pretending to comprehend and englobe the analytic register, to posit their own extraterritoriality in relation to psychoanalysis. Whence, for example, the title of a recent French essay, "La psychanalyse dans le matérialisme historique," and its project: to constitute psychoanalysis as a "regional theory" within the "continent of historical materialism."[2]

,And yet, to begin these reflections by evoking a chance repetition of the word *unheimlich* is to recall that the "analytic"—which, according to Freud, came increasingly to bear the imprint of the "uncanny"— tends to irrupt precisely where it shouldn't, in a certain exterritoriality that wrenches analysis outside of itself. For one might well evolve the following thesis from the text on the uncanny: what is *unheimlich* about the *unheimlich* is that absolutely *anything* can be *unheimlich*.[3] The term *anything* is eloquent with arbitrariness and impropriety; it suggests that what is electively

2. Michel Tort, in *Nouvelle Revue de Psychanalyse,* I (1970), p. 152.

3. See my *"Poe pourri:* Lacan's Purloined Letter" in *Semiotexte,* III (1975).

available to contamination by the *unheimlich* would seem so fundamentally extrinsic to it as to be designated as its other: *Heimlichkeit*. *Everything* would thus be vulnerable to seizure by that repetitive and disruptive movement even as, in the homologous Freudian thesis of "pansexualism," every activity—anything —may become the occasion of a "marginal" emergence of sexuality. In fact, the point of departure of the French reading of Freud at its most virulent has been the willingness not to exclude from that totality the theoretical discourse of Freud himself, whose readability would thus presuppose the elaboration of a fantasmatics of metapsychology: whence a certain collapse of the very possibility of metalanguage.

Let us return to the Marxian *exterior*. For our aim in these pages will be to delineate a *failed* exit from the Freudian register into Marx's text, and specifically into the three principal works concerned with revolution in France (*Class Struggles in France, The Eighteenth Brumaire of Louis Bonaparte, The Civil War in France*). I speak of failure since I present a reading which by no means set out to be Freudian, which initially was a search for a realm of inquiry extrinsic to the analytic, but which came to be infiltrated increasingly, ineluctably, by a certain Freudian problematic insistent within—or between—Marx's texts. A failed leave then, but also what that failure—as a transformative reading of three texts of Marx—has succeeded in accomplishing. What follows then is by no means a psychologization of the political, but something stranger and more disquieting: a fantasmatization of several of the crucial texts through which the history of the West has been most forcefully thematized.

An initial danger entailed by this style of reading would be to revert to a position analogous to that attributed by Marx and Engels in the *Manifesto* to "critical utopian" socialists: "social activity is to yield to their personal ingeniousness, historical conditions of emancipation to imaginary ones."[4] The imposition from above of various interpretative grids, the "application" of psychoanalysis would in this case be regrettable or fruitless. These pages would seek, then, instead to coincide with a certain intertextual stratum—or "social activity [*gesellschaftliche Tätigkeit*]"—in Marx which is itself generative of the uncanny, liberatory of energy. Now it may be that rediscovering a certain Freud within Marx is itself *unheimlich,* for the uncanny for Freud is thought of above all in terms of repetition-as-failure. But then the site of that rediscovery, within one of the crucial texts on revolution in France, is precisely that of a traumatic repetition within history (and, we shall see, within Marx's theory as well), an utterly new kind of catastrophe, the return of a Bonaparte: "clumsily cunning, knavishly naive, doltishly sublime, calculated superstition, pathetic burlesque, cleverly stupid anachronism, a world historical piece of buffoonery, an undecipherable hieroglyphic for the understanding of the civilized . . ." (p. 44). Our failed encounter with Marx's text shall thus have repeated Marx's failed engagement with history. The project, it may be objected, is laughable, even farcical. But that repetition and that failure are, of course, characterized in precisely those terms in

4. "Manifest der Kommunistischen Partei" in *Werke,* IV (Berlin: Dietz Verlag, 1969), p. 490.

Marx's text: "Hegel remarks somewhere that all great events and historical personages occur, as it were, twice. He forgot to add: the first time as tragedy, the second as farce" (p. 115).[5]

We shall thus be concerned with a certain form of laughter in its relation to a specific type of parasite, or rather with a certain *fissioning* of Marx's laughter and with a transformation within what may no longer be quite designated as his *concept* of the parasite.

As early as his first article on the events of February–June 1848, in the *Neue Rheinische Zeitung,* Marx envisaged history—and quintessentially the history of the revolution—as a dialectical movement progressing through reversals and tending, in a totalizing advance, toward the elimination of every parasite of the revolution. Reversal: "Revolutionary advance made headway not by its immediate tragi-comic conquests, but on the contrary by the creation of an opponent, by fighting whom the party of revolt first ripened into a real revolutionary party" (p. 11). The negativity which gnaws at and motivates history is utterly subordinate to an invincible positivity. The "monstrous defeat of June (1848)," by revealing with stunning clarity the conflicts dividing capitalist society, is in the service of the revolution and already pregnant with "victory" (p. 21). The tragic revelation born of the June massacre can culminate only in a

5. References in the text to *The Eighteenth Brumaire of Louis Bonaparte* are to the German edition: *Der achtzehnte Brumaire des Louis Bonaparte* in *Werke,* VIII (Berlin: Dietz Verlag, 1960). The translation, occasionally modified, is that of International Publishers.

dialectical reversal which this time will accomplish the truth of History so utterly that the events of June are already thinkable in the light of that conclusion. "And we cry: The revolution is dead! Long live the revolution!" (p. 34).

Now the history under consideration proceeds by devouring the parasites that pretend to live off of it. For already on the first page of *Class Struggles in France,* we encounter, in the margins of the revolution, a second kind of negativity which the revolution will be equally—though differently—obliged to neutralize and which Marx calls "the traditional pre-revolutionary appendages [*vorrevolutionären traditionnellen Anhängsel*]" (p. 11). Since Bonapartism will later be conceived of as a generalized parasitism, we shall do well to locate the insistence of a certain parasitism already in the years before *The Eighteenth Brumaire* and of the laughter it elicits. The "appendage" in this case appears as a simulacrum of revolution, grotesque in its pretention to pass itself off as the real thing. More specifically, it is identified with the *(petit bourgeois)* politics of the Montagne whose climactic—and catastrophic—*day* is dated June 13, 1849. Marx summarizes the events culminating in June 13, in *The Eighteenth Brumaire,* as follows:

The bombardment of Rome by the French troops . . . violated Article V of the Constitution which forbids the French republic to employ its military forces against the freedom of another people. In addition, Article IV prohibited any declaration of war on the part of the executive power without the assent of the National Assembly, and by its resolution of May 8, the Constituent Assembly had disapproved of the Roman expedition. On these grounds Ledru-Rollin brought in a bill of impeachment against Bonaparte and his ministers on June 11, 1849. Exasperated by the stings of Thiers, he actually let himself be carried away to the point of threatening that he would defend the Constitution by every means, even with arms in hand. The Montagne rose to a man and repeated this call to arms. On June 12, the National Assembly rejected the bill of impeachment, and the Montagne left the parliament. The events of June 13 are known: the proclamation by the section of the Montagne, declaring Bonaparte and his ministers "outside the Constitution"; the street procession of the democratic National Guards, who, unarmed as they were, dispersed on encountering the troops of Changarnier, etc., etc. A part of the Montagne fled abroad; another part was arraigned before the High Court at Bourges, and a parliamentary regulation subjected the remainder to the school-masterly surveillance of the President of the National Assembly. Paris was again declared in a state of siege and the democratic part of its National Guard dissolved. Thus the influence of the Montagne in parliament and the power of the *petits bourgeois* in Paris were broken. (p. 143)

The day of June 13 was to remain for Marx a constant point of reference. More than twenty years later, during the Paris Commune, he would write to Kugelmann: "I am absolutely incapable of understanding how you can compare the *petit bourgeois* demonstrations *à la* June 1849, etc., with the current struggle in Paris."[6] But already, in the midst of the events, the effort of political analysis consisted in a differentiation of the ludicrous simulacrum of revolution from what it merely imitated. "June 1849 was a caricature, as

6. Letter of 17 April 1871, in *Werke,* XXXIII (Berlin: Dietz Verlag, 1966), p. 209.

laughable as it was futile, of June 1848." And Marx
continues: "In June 1848, the constituent bourgeois
republic, by an unspeakable blow against the proletariat, in June 1849, the constituted bourgeois republic, by an unutterable *comedy* with the *petite bourgeoisie,*
had inscribed itself in the birth-register of history. June
1849 was the nemesis of June 1848 . . . June 1849 was
not a bloody *tragedy* between wage-labor and capital,
but a prison-filling and lamentable play of debtors and
creditors" (p. 63). Tragedy/comedy. The tactic has
been to reduce the "appendage" by forcing it into a
position of antithesis in order better to envelop it. Such
are the ruses and the laughter of dialectic. But it is a
laughter which quickly subsides to the extent that the
comic here is defined as a ludicrous imitation of the
tragic and eventually comes to be absorbed, through
the movement of the analysis, by the latter instance.

Whereupon there emerge a third genre—farce—
and a different mode of laughter which cannot be reduced, which figures, as we shall see, the degree zero of
reductionism. For Marx this farcical instance is
Bonapartism. It inaugurates a local collapse of history,
a repetitive span which opens a veritable cesura in
time: "An entire people, which had imagined that by
means of a revolution it had imparted to itself an accel-
erated power of motion, suddenly finds itself set back
into a defunct epoch and, in order that no doubt as to
the relapse may be possible, the old dates rise again, the
old chronology, the old names, the old edicts, which
had long become a subject of antiquarian erudition,
and the old minions of the law, who had seemed long
decayed" (p. 117). Emptied of its dialectical content,

history seems "without events," that is, barely history, "wearing with constant repetition of the same tensions, the same relaxations" (p. 136). For it is as though the movement of dialectic had been frozen. Whereas the *higher* was inevitably to be overthrown by the *lower*—the *bourgeoisie* by the proletariat—those two poles remain constant and are mutually impoverished by a strange irruption of something lower than the low . . . at the top. For Bonaparte seems to short-circuit both dialectic and class struggle in gathering in his service the "scum (*Auswurf*), offal (*Abfall*), refuse (*Abhub*) of all classes," the *lumpen-proletariat* (p. 161).

We would suggest at this juncture that for Marx as writer *The Eighteenth Brumaire* is above all the site where that heterogeneity, in its unassimilability to every dialectical totalization, is *affirmed*. For the exhilaration, the almost Rabelaisian verve of the following inventory of the Bonapartist Société du 10 Décembre is surely a crucial index: "Alongside decayed *roués* with dubious means of subsistence and dubious origin [*von zweideutiger Herkunft*], alongside ruined and reckless cast-offs of the *bourgeoisie,* were vagabonds, discharged soldiers, discharged jailbirds, escaped galley-slaves, swindlers, impostors, *lazzaroni,* pickpockets, bamboozlers, gamblers, *maquereaux,* brothel keepers, porters, literary hacks, organ-grinders, ragpickers, knife-grinders, tinkers, beggars—in short, the whole amorphous disintegrated mass of flotsom and jetsom the French call *la bohème*" (p. 161). A certain proliferating energy is thus released within Marx's writing upon contact with the Bonapartist instance. It generates the motley cast of the Marxian *farce,* a genre which excites a different kind of laughter than (*petit bourgeois*) comedy, and which, in its absurdity, elicits tears unknown to (proletarian) tragedy, free of every promise of redemption. The history of a grotesque repetition thus comes to be marked by the repetitive insistence of a specific structure: a specular—or reversible—relation is exceeded by a heterogeneous, negatively charged instance whose situation is one of deviation or displacement in relation to one of the poles of the initial opposition. The dialectic between *bourgeoisie* and proletariat is congealed to the advantage of the subproletariat. The relation subordinating *petit bourgeois* comedy to proletarian tragedy gives way to Bonapartist farce. The three terms might even be distributed temporally as a function of the historic days on which they surface most forcefully: June 23, 1848, June 13, 1849, each the "classically pure expression [*Ausdruck*]" of the class contributing to it; finally, December 2, 1851, which seems a point of breakage with the metaphorics of expression itself (*Class Struggles,* p. 69).

For the Bonapartist instance, even as it constitutes a scandal in history, is no less one within Marx's discourse to the extent that it entails a break with the notion of class representation. One might indeed imagine a development which would bring the reader from an illusory notion of the State as the representative of all of society to its more adequate concept as the representative of a specific class in the exploitation of a different one. Such was the reading of the State proposed by the *Manifesto:* "The executive of the modern state [*die moderne Staatsgewalt*] is but a committee for managing the common affairs [*gemeinschaftlichen Ge-*

schäfte] of the whole *bourgeoisie."* And such will be the lesson drawn by Lenin from his reading of Marx: "According to Marx, the State is an organ of class *domination,* an organ of *oppression* of one class by another."[7]

And yet the piquancy of Bonapartism lies entirely in the emergence of a State which has been emptied of its class content. For if the particularity of Bonaparte is to incarnate the State "in its antagonism with Society," that State can no longer represent a segment of the Society and participate—as exploiter or exploited—in its conflicts.[8] Bonaparte is "the executive power become independent" of Society (p. 204). He has no other existence than his extravagant capacity to figure a *different* mode of counter-revolution: "he is somebody solely by dint of having broken the political power of the middle class and by breaking it daily anew." Or rather, he is the vehicle through which the crucial notion of class interest comes undone: "this *bourgeoisie,* which every moment sacrificed its general class interests, its political interests, to the narrowest and most sordid private interests . . ." (p. 185).

Bonapartism thus figures the intersection of two parasitisms, that of the *lumpen-proletariat* and that of the State *per se*: "this appalling parasitic body, which enmeshes the body of French society like a net and chokes all its pores" (p. 196). But if it is a form of rot within history, it is no less so, we would suggest, in

7. *The State and Revolution* (Peking: Foreign Language Press, 1965), p. 8.

8. "The Rule of the Pretorians" in *New York Tribune,* March 12, 1858, quoted in M. Rubel, *Marx devant le bonapartisme* (The Hague: Mouton, 1960), p. 50.

Marxist theory. For what is the status of a State that no
longer represents anything? The efforts to mend or
circumscribe this breach begin with Marx himself:
"only under the second Bonaparte does the state seem
to have made itself completely independent . . . . And
yet the state power is not suspended in mid air.
Bonaparte represents a class and the most numerous
class of French society at that, the *small-holding (Parzel-
len) peasants*" (p. 197). And yet however distrustful
Marx may be of the notion of an antagonism between
State and Society, his analysis eventually constrains
him to admit that, in relation to the peasantry,
Bonapartism offers only a semblance of representation. For Louis Bonaparte represents the peasants only
in the electoral mode, and consequently their class
interests are by no means represented by him. And if
Bonapartism irrupts within history as a "crude peasant
joke [*einen schnöden Bauernwitz*]," it must be admitted
that the peasants, by supporting the nephew a half-
century after the policies of the uncle have stopped
conforming to their class interest, are as much the vic-
tims as the perpetrators of the joke (*Class Struggles*, p.
46). "All the 'idées napoléoniennes' *are ideas of the unde-
veloped small-holding* [*Parzelle*], *in the freshness of its
youth*. For the *Parzelle* that has outlived its day they are
an absurdity, the mere hallucinations of its death
struggle . . ." (p. 203). Thus the invocation of the
small-holding peasantry by no means reduces the
break with representation. In Marx's *Witz* (which is
already farce), as in Freud's, the process of disruption is
remarkably different from that transpiring in the re-

stricted register of comedy.[9] We should take care not to confuse the laughter of June 13 with that of December 2.

A second effort to reduce the scandal of Bonapartism for Marxian discourse may be observed in the efforts of a leading academic expert on Marx, Maximilien Rubel. Thus at the end of his meticulous reading of the entirety of Marx's journalism on Bonapartism, Rubel seems intent on saving Marx from his own conclusions.

Mais la domination statique de l'Etat sur la Société est une conception irrecevable. Il faut comprendre qu'ici Marx, dialecticien, raisonne plutôt qu'il ne décrit, et raisonne en perspective. Il ne lui a pas échappé que derrière les hommes . . . c'est l'Etat comme tel qu'il faut dévisager: il repose "sur la contradiction entre la vie publique et la vie privée, sur la contradiction entre les intérêts généraux et les intérêts particuliers . . . l'existence de l'Etat et de la servitude sont inséparables." Des formes intermédiaires sont observables, entre *l'idée* de l'Etat et, en l'occurrence, le *bonapartisme* (illustration historique de cette *idée*): *l'Etat bourgeois* en soi, le régime parlementaire. Cette dernière forme, dit Marx, contient en germe l'Etat bonapartiste. L'Etat, création de la Société, s'en détache et la domine: c'est aussi ce que nous savons, par Marx, du Capital et du Travail. Le lien méthodique entre l'Etat et le Capital, voila l'idée véritablement marxienne que l'Adresse sur la Commune nous livrera.[10]

9. For a discussion of the implications of the distinction *Witz*/comedy in Freud, see my "How to Read Freud on Jokes: The Critic as *Schadchen,*" *New Literary History,* Spring (1975).
10. Rubel, p. 156.

We too shall eventually come to read—however differently—the Address on the Commune. At this juncture, we shall simply observe in Rubel's remarks a certain pressure intent on blunting the acuteness of the Bonapartist farce. Marx's stance on Bonapartism and, implicitly, against the pertinence of the concept of representation is not to be read, we are told, as a "description" of reality and, consequently, as a representation of truth. For it plays havoc with what is hastily termed "the true Marxian idea" of the State. Whereupon we encounter a passage on mediation whose aim seems to be to force what Marx calls the 'hieroglyph" of Bonapartism back into its matrix or "germ," the parliamentary regime. There is, then, a strange analogy between this academic reading of Marx's theory—mitigating every "Bonapartist" threat to the philosophical category of representation, preventing any emancipation of a parasitism calling into question the subordination of parasite (State, Capital) to the body (Society, Labor) sustaining it—and the political project of the Constituent Assembly of 1848: "hailing in the (presidential) *homunculus* of the constitution the son of his mother" (*Class Struggles,* p. 43). In Marx's text, in the text of history, a single answer comes to obstruct both endeavors: "Futile precautions [*Vergebliche Vorkehrungen*]! The first day of the realization of the constitution was the last day of the rule of the Constituent Assembly. At the bottom of the ballot box lay its sentence of death. It sought 'the son of his mother' and found 'the nephew of his uncle' " (*Class Struggles,* p. 44). Such would be the irreducible perversity of a certain Oedipal configuration insistent on the theoretico-historical scene of Europe.

Thus, in both Marx and in the Marxologists there is a pressure to restrict what is liberated in *The Eighteenth Brumaire* under the rubric of Bonapartism. Before interrogating a third case of resistence to that instance, before examining what light is cast on our enigma by the Address on the Commune, we may already posit a first reading of our problem. For from the very beginning of our inquiry, we have continuously encountered in—and with—Marx's text the repetitive insistence of a specific structure: the irruption of a *third* element which in its heterogeneity, asymmetry, and unexpectedness, breaks the unity of two specular terms and rots away their *closure*. In—or rather, outside—the class struggle, against Marx's expectation, we observed the *lumpen-proletariat* irrupting at the summit of society once the massacres of June 1848 had eliminated any possibility of a reversal of the *bourgeoisie* by the proletariat. Spatially, the configuration may be read in terms of a strange agitation—or (upward) mobility—of the "more-than-low" while the "top" and "bottom" remain in place. Distributed in time, we find the interminable pseudo-event of December 2, 1851, monopolizing Marx's attention at the expense of the—appalling or ludicrous—events of June 23, 1848, and June 13, 1849. In terms of the classical categories of poetics, we encounter a splitting of comic laughter into farce, a genre opposed quite differently—than comedy—to tragedy. Now within Marx's theory, but already breaking with a certain stratum of it, we see the project of advancing from a *deluded* notion of the relation of representation between State and Society to a *true* notion of that relation—the State as instrument of exploitation of one class by another—give way to an affirmation of an antagonism between State and Society and consequently of the *irrevelance* of the category of (true or false) representation. But may we not, then, read this instance, which breaks, say, with the *philosopheme of representation* (and, consequently, of truth), and which is homologous, through its asymmetry and heterogeneity, with all the other "third terms" active in the text, as the formation in the text most alive to what never ceases recurring within it: to the fact that in an *unheimlich* manner, absolutely *anything* may come to occupy the positions of the repetitive structure?

The full bearing of that thesis will become apparent shortly. But already we may delineate certain of its transformative effects on "Bonapartism" within Marx's text. Thus, on two occasions, Marx takes his distance from his own tendency to see in Louis Bonaparte a mere parody of Napoleon, the parasite of his greatness. First, in a letter of February 14, 1858, to Engels: "In point of fact, he is not only Napoléon le Petit, in Victor Hugo's sense, that is, the antithesis of Napoléon le Grand: he personifies even more, and quite marvelously, the pettiness of the great Napoleon." Then in the *New York Tribune* on April 27 of the same year: "When Victor Hugo called the nephew 'Napoléon le Petit,' he acknowledged the greatness of the uncle. The title of his famous diatribe expressed an antithesis and, to a certain degree, he subscribed to that cult of Napoleon on which the son of Hortense de Beauharnais has succeeded in erecting the bloody system of his fortune. It would be more useful to have the present generation admit that Napoléon le Petit

figures, in fact, the pettiness of Napoléon le Grand."
Marx's reading is thus situated somewhere beyond the
antithesis *(petit/grand)*, in a certain pettiness which was
always already at work in undermining "greatness"
from within. But if, within the antithesis, Napoleon III
is "petit" above all through his incapacity to be anything but an imitation or degraded representation of
Napoleon I, his simulacrum, access to the realm beyond the antithesis simultaneously entails leaving the
domain of representation. Marx's Bonapartism becomes a generalized parasitism, ultimately excluding
the very possibility of a pre-parasitic presence. Such
would be the revenge wreaked on dialectics by all
those "appendages [*Anhängsel*]" which the dialectics of
history seemed intent on neutralizing through assimilation.

To read *The Eighteenth Brumaire of Louis Bonaparte* as
the systematic dispersion of the philosopheme of representation is, as well, to take up Marx's own analytic
technique at its most concrete. Thus, in his reading of
the royalist ideologies prior to the *coup d'état,* Marx
writes: "The *parliamentary republic* was more than the
neutral territory on which the two factions of the
French *bourgeoisie,* Legitimists and Orleanists, large
landed property and industry, could dwell side by side
with equality of rights. It was the unavoidable condition of their *common* rule, the sole form of state in
which their general class interest subjected to itself
both the claims of their particular factions and all the
remaining classes of society. As royalists they fell back
into their old antagonism . . ." (p. 177). The Legitimist
and Orleanist ideologies, in their incompatibility,

function together as a specular system working in the service of a process of repression. But what is repressed is by no means a synthesis of the two positions or a compromise between their contents. For the "content" *represented* in and by each ideology exists only in order to repress or mask a "desire"—for the parliamentary republic—which is entirely incompatible with that content. Thus, for Marx as analyst—as for us as readers of Marx—reading entails endeavoring to affirm a tertiary instance breaking with the registers of specularity and representation. It is the degree zero of polysemy, the fundamentally *heterogenizing* movement of dissemination.[11]

A third effort to reduce the "Bonapartist" instance appears in a brief unpublished text prepared for the Collège de Sociologie Sacrée by Georges Bataille.[12] "Dès qu'il s'agit des structures principales, les marxistes ou se dérobent ou introduisent des définitions nouvelles désastreuses. Je ne citerai que l'introduction par Trotski de la notion de bonapartisme, qui à elle seule suffit à marquer le peu de résistance que l'habitude de considérer la matière sociale offre à la monstruosité: le bonapartisme trotskiste ne recouvre-t-il pas, sous le même vocable, entre les deux Napoléons qui ont régné, Bismarck, Staline, Von Papen et le défunt président Doumergue?" To attack the term "Bonapartism" as a Trotskyist "monstrosity" is plainly an act of denial. Bataille's rage against

11. See Jacques Derrida, *La Dissémination* (Paris: Seuil, 1972).
12. My thanks to Denis Hollier for having indicated this text to me. It will appear shortly in an anthology of works of the Collège de Sociologie Sacrée that he is preparing.

"Bonapartism" continues: "Jamais des échafaudages verbaux aussi vides n'ont été employés à égarer les passions." The result: "notre existence aujourd'hui [est] une absurdité et [sera] demain une pourriture." The only acceptable antidote to these "extravagances": "la démarche sans éclat de la science . . . employer des mots qui aient la précision des instruments de chirurgie." For "une science qui se définit et entre en jeu est tout d'abord souffrance et dure réserve autant que certitude de vaincre."

Concerning Bataille's text, we would offer a series of remarks regarding, first of all, the precision with which the author, even as he opposes it, has delineated certain crucial traits of "Bonapartism" as we have elaborated them in Marx's text: a "monstrosity" in theory; a form of rot ("pourriture") within the reality of history; a break with the truth of representation ("jamais des échafaudages verbaux aussi vides . . . "). That degree of exactitude, however, should not surprise us to the extent that Marx's "Bonapartism," in its heterogeneity, in the repulsion and anxious laughter elicited by the endless and obscene orgies of the *lumpen* of the Société du 10 Décembre, strikes us as being strangely akin to the problematic of Bataille. We would suggest that the *matter* of materialism at work within and upon human subjectivity finds its precise point of insertion in Marx's text in the *excesses* of the Bonapartists. Or rather, it is as though Marx's "Bonapartism" were the "pineal eye" of capitalism. Compare the two texts. Marx: "The Constitution, made inviolable in so ingenious a manner, was nevertheless, like Achilles, vulnerable in one point, not

in the heel, but in the head, or rather in the two heads
in which it was to squander itself—the *Legislative Assembly,* on the one hand, the *President,* on the other" (p.
127). Bataille: " . . . lorsque j'imaginais la possibilité
déconcertante de l'oeil pinéal, je n'avais pas d'autre
intention que de représenter des dégagements d'éner-
gie au sommet du crâne aussi crus que ceux qui rendent
si horrible à voir la protubérance anale de quelques
singes . . . cet oeil que j'avais voulu avoir au sommet
du crâne . . . ne m'apparaissait pas autrement que
comme un organe sexuel d'une sensibilité inouïe, qui
aurait vibré en me faisant pousser des cris atroces, les
cris d'une éjaculation grandiose mais puante . . . ."
And further on: "je me représentais l'oeil au sommet
du crâne comme un horrible volcan en éruption,
justement avec le caractère louche et comique qui s'at-
tache au derrière et à ses excrétions."[13] In Marx's
"Bonapartism," then, as in Bataille's "pineal eye,"
there is a displacement of an extremely *base* form of
heterogeneity to the top, and, concomitantly, a loss of
control—Bataille: of the head; Marx: in the heads—in
a catastrophically repetitive *skid.* The two instances
strangely combine the "sinister (*louche*)" and the
"comic" (or "farcical") and even the repulsive and
scatological: through the "bordello" side of the Société
du 10 Décembre, through the metaphorics of *waste*
that comes to invest it, and above all, perhaps, through
one's growing sense, upon reading *The Eighteenth
Brumaire,* that Marx must have lived the history of
France from 1848 to 1852—the revolution careening

13. *Oeuvres complètes,* II (Paris: Gallimard, 1970), p. 14.

backwards—as resembling nothing so much as a la-
trine backing up . . .

Ultimately our "fantasmatics of history" in Marx
coincides so extensively with Bataille's "mythological
anthropology" that one has the impression that in
"repressing" Marx's Bonapartism, Bataille is rejecting his own problematic. That suspicion is confirmed
when we observe Bataille quite uncharacteristically
invoking "la démarche sans éclat de la science" and
a "dure réserve" against the Bonapartist "monstruosité." As an appeal to "la réserve" against . . .
a radical expenditure, Bataille's text thus recognizes
and represses Marx's Bonapartism, failing in the process to exploit one of the densest regions of potential
articulation between the writings of the two authors.

We shall turn briefly now to a second text by
Bataille—"*La vieille taupe* et le préfixe *sur* dans les mots
surhomme et *surréalisme*"—in which the encounter with
"Bonapartism" will once again go awry—though in a
symmetrical manner. For to delineate the structure of
that symmetry or specularity will allow us better to
grasp what exceeds it in Marx. Once again, but more
markedly, what is at stake is a conflict between the *high*
and the *low*:

L'idéalisme révolutionnaire tend à faire de la révolution un
aigle au-dessus des aigles, un *suraigle* abattant les im-
périalismes autoritaires, une idée aussi radieuse qu'un ado-
lescent s'emparant éloquemment du pouvoir au bénéfice
d'une illumination utopique. Cette déviation aboutit
naturellement à l'échec de la révolution et à la satisfaction du
besoin éminent d'idéalisme à l'aide d'un fascisme militaire.
L'épopée napoléonienne en est le développement le moins

dérisoire: une révolution icarienne châtrée, l'impérialisme
éhonté exploitant l'impulsion révolutionnaire . . . . Cepen-
dant ramenée à l'action souterraine des faits économiques la
révolution 'vieille taupe' creuse des galeries dans un sol dé-
composé et répugnant pour le nez délicat des utopistes.
'Vieille taupe,' dans la bouche de Marx, expression bruy-
ante d'une pleine satisfaction du tressaillement révolutionnaire des masses est à mettre en rapport avec la notion de
soulèvement géologique telle qu'elle est exprimée dans le
Manifeste communiste. Le point de départ de Marx n'a rien à
voir avec le ciel, lieu d'élection de l'aigle impérialiste comme
des utopies chrétiennes ou révolutionnaires. Il se situe dans
les entrailles du sol, comme dans les entrailles matérialistes
des prolétaires.[14]

In this case, then, the "rot (*pourriture*)"—which appears in an epigraph drawn from Marx—would be
affirmed against the imperialist movement of sublima-
tion: the "old mole" against the eagle. The "difficult
reserve [*dure réserve*]," here explicitly Fascist, is abandoned in favor of what was described in the unpublished text in terms of "monstruosité" and "extravagances." And yet in *The Eighteenth Brumaire of Louis
Bonaparte,* the relation between old mole and imperial
eagle is by no means one of simple opposition: "But
the revolution is thoroughgoing. It is still journeying
through purgatory. It does its work methodically. By
December 2, 1851, it had completed one half of its
preparatory work; it is now completing the other half.
First it perfected the parliamentary power, in order to
be able to overthrow it. Now that it has attained this, it
perfects the *executive* power, reduces it to its purest
expression, isolates it, sets it up against itself as the sole

14. *Ibid.,* p. 97.

target, in order to concentrate all its forces of destruction against it. And when it has done this second half of
its preliminary work, Europe will leap from its seat
and exultantly exclaim: Well grubbed, old mole! " (p.
196). The relation between burrowing mole and eagle
is thus one of inscription rather than opposition. We
would suggest that the eagle is the form assumed by
the hieroglyph traced by the mole. The eagle would
figure a restricted economy within the general
economy constituted by the tracks—and tunnels—of
the mole. The mole engenders and *wills* the eagle but
also wishes to dismantle it. But that dismantling cannot be accomplished in any *confrontation* for the simple
reason that the Bonapartist eagle, as we have seen, is
the precipitating focus of everything *most base*. We
should perhaps think of the eagle's defeat as a kind of
volatilization at the very moment that the eagle—to
whom, according to "L'oeil pinéal," the ancients attributed "la faculté de contempler le soleil face à face",
which lives then in the very medium of confrontation—is shown to be through and through a mirage
generated by the mole, by a supplement, or excess, of
his burrowing.[15]

The "old mole," then, cannot desire the eagle in the
same way that the dialectic seemed to desire the
counter-revolution of June 1848. Above all because the
eagle is not an anti-mole. At this juncture, we approach
the question of the relation between Marx/Bataille and
Hegel (Derrida: "Son nom est si étrange. De l'aigle il
tient la puissance impériale ou historique. Ceux qui le
prononcent encore à la française, il y en a, ne sont

15. *Ibid.,* p. 14.

ridicules que jusqu'à un certain point . . .").[16] For if
the general economy of Bataille, in Derrida's phrase,
figures a Hegelianism *sans réserve,* Marx's Bonapartism, we would suggest, repeating the paradox, offers
the image of a capitalism *sans réserve.*[17]

This is so first of all by virtue of the high-farcical
generalization of *bourgeois* violence, which no longer
seems to spare any instance in the dialectic of history
and strikes electively—such is the piquancy of Bonapartism—the *bourgeoisie* itself: "And, finally, the
high priests of 'religion and order' themselves are
driven with kicks from their Pythian tripods, hauled
out of their beds in the darkness of night, put in
prison-vans, thrown into dungeons or sent into exile;
their temple is razed, their mouths sealed, their pens
broken, their law torn to pieces, all in the name of
religion, property, family, order. Middle-class fanatics
of order are shot down on their balconies by mobs of
drunken soldiers, the sanctity of their homes profaned,
their houses bombed for amusement—in the name of
property, family, religion, and order" (p. 123). The
system of (parliamentary) representation, the system
of (ideological, philosophical) representations of the
bourgeoisie, with all the *minor* risks they entail, culminate against every expectation in a situation where the
mastery of the master-class is demolished through the
very processes whose sole function had been the
maintenance of that mastery. History skids off course;
dialectic is ruinously squandered; Marx vents his hilar-

16. *Glas* (Paris: Galilée, 1974), p. 7.
17. "De l'économie restreinte à l'économie générale" in *L'Ecri-
ture et la Différence* (Paris: Seuil, 1967), p. 369.

ity: "Finally, the scum of *bourgeois* society forms the *holy phalanx of order* and the hero Crapulinski installs himself in the Tuileries as the "savior of society" (p. 123).

Bracketing the political question, we may affirm that *in its structure,* the intervention of Bataille within Hegel's system repeats the irruption of Marx's Bonapartism within the dialectic of history. To which end, we need but quote a remarkable paragraph of Derrida concerning Bataille's reading of Hegel:

Hegel avait clairement énoncé la nécessité pour le maître de garder la vie qu'il expose. Sans cette économie de la vie, la "suprême preuve par le moyen de la mort supprime en même temps la certitude de soi-même en général." Aller au-devant de la mort pure et simple, c'est donc risquer la perte absolue du sens, dans la mesure où celui-ci passe nécessairement par la vérité du maître et la conscience de soi. On risque de perdre l'effet, le bénéfice de sens que l'on voulait gagner au jeu. Cette mort pure et simple, cette mort muette et sans rendement, Hegel l'appelait *négativité abstraite,* par opposition à la "négation de la conscience qui supprime de telle façon qu'elle *conserve* et *retient* ce qui est supprimé" et qui "par là même survit au fait de devenir supprimé . . . . Dans cette expérience, la conscience de soi apprend que la Vie lui est aussi essentielle que la pure conscience de soi . . . ." Eclat de rire de Bataille . . . .[18]

And that hilarity—of/at dialectics—is prolonged in a strange movement which exacerbates and exceeds the Hegelian system:

"La tache aveugle du hégélianisme, autour de laquelle peut s'organiser la représentation du sens, c'est ce point où la

18. *Ibid.,* pp. 375–376.

destruction, la suppression, la mort, le sacrifice constituent une dépense si irréversible, une négativité si radicale—il faut dire ici *sans réserve*—qu'on ne peut même plus les déterminer en négativité dans un procès ou système . . . .[19]

Thus in the *jeu majeur* of Bataille, as in the Bonapartism of Marx, mastery, representation, and the toiling totality of dialectic are all *dilapidated* by a passage to the limit.

Now this passage to the limit is, of course, thematized by Bataille in terms of *expenditure (dépense)*. And since the first page of "La Notion de Dépense" alludes manifestly to Freud ("des principes que l'on cherche à situer au-delà de l'utile et du plaisir"), we shall in turn, in these prolegomena to a genealogy of the notion of expenditure in Bataille, interrogate a further realm—in Freud—beyond the pleasure principle: the death instinct (*Todestrieb*). And indeed, as our texts proliferate, we shall have increasingly the feeling, in this reading of Marx, of circulating in an *unheimliche Anonymität,* of working against the press law of 1850.

But what instance in Marx might correspond to the notion of *dépense* in Bataille and to that absolute discharge/expenditure of tensions figured by the death instinct? Within *The Eighteenth Brumaire of Louis Bonaparte,* we would situate such a formation in the fiscal policy of the future Napoleon III, informed as it was by "the entire financial science of the *lumpenproletariat*" (p. 154). For Bonaparte, "raised on the shield [*auf den Schild gehoben*] by a drunken soldiery, which he has bought with liquor and sausages, and

19. *Ibid.,* p. 380.

which he must continually ply [werfen] with sausage anew,"
was able to survive, according to Marx, only by pur-
chasing the support of his partisans, by accumulating
disastrous debts as a result of his unproductive extravagances (p. 197). Thus, when Marx's Bonapartism
thinks its own existence, it gives way to a pseudo-
science of expenditure, a simulacrum of science: "the
entire financial science of the *lumpen-proletariat.*"

Now the situation of this Bonapartist simulacrum of
science—linked to the heterogeneous instance of
expenditure—in Marx's text leads us to think of a second pseudo-science, or "hydraulics," of absolute expenditure or discharge in Freud. For the death instinct
per se remains the segment of Freud's work least as-
similable not only by various positivist accommoda-
tions of psychoanalysis, but by the previous Freudian
problematic which its emergence all but shattered.
(How, for example, might one think in "economic
terms" of the reduction of tensions as an increase in
pain?) From a perspective currently quite common (at
least outside of France), the "science" of psychoanalysis feels as justified in rejecting Freud's discourse
on absolute discharge as . . . Marx, for example,
in refusing the Bonapartist discourse—or practice
—of ruinous expenditure. And yet a rigorous reading
of Freud's text has succeeded in delineating a certain
necessity of the death instinct.[20] For that fundamental principle of repetition is itself, in its structure,
the repetition of what in the *Project* of 1895 had been

20. See in particular Jean Laplanche, *Vie et mort en psychanalyse*
(Paris: Flammarion, 1970), Chapter VI: "Pourquoi la pulsion de
mort?"

called the "principle of neuronic inertia" and would
later become the "pleasure principle." And whatever the biological fantasia accompanying the hypothesis of a death instinct, what the absolute discharge of tensions originally referred to was the total
evacuation of affect from ideational representative to
ideational representative in dreams and hysterical
symptoms: that is, the fact of unconscious displacement or "primary process' thinking. The example
given by Freud himself in the *Project* may prove useful
here. He writes first of the "normal" functioning of the
psyche:"Symbols are formed in this way normally as
well. A soldier will sacrifice himself for a piece of col-
oured cloth on a pole, because it has become the symbol of his native country; and no one considers this
neurotic . . . . The knight who fights for a lady's glove
knows, in the first place, that the glove owes its impor-
tance to the lady; and, secondly, his worship of the
glove does not in the least prevent him from thinking
of the lady and serving her in other ways."[21] Laplanche
comments: "Ainsi dans ces deux exemples de symbole
'normal,' ce qui nous éloigne de l'hystérie, c'est que le
souvenir du symbolisé reste présent, que le symbolisé
reste investi; sinon nous nous trouverions devant cette
absurdité (qui n'est d'ailleurs pas inimaginable!): un
soldat capable de mourir pour le drapeau, un chevalier
servant se sacrifiant pour le gant, en oubliant com-
plètement la patrie ou la dame qui se trouvent derrière
ces symboles."[22] Now it is this second situation, with

21. "Project for a Scientific Psychology" in *The Origins of
Psychoanalysis* (New York: Basic Books, 1954), p. 407.
22. Laplanche, *Vie et mort en psychanalyse,* p. 66.

the complement of devastating—or depleting—
implications that it entails for the very category of
representation, that is at stake in Freud's discourse on
absolute discharge. The "hysterical" sacrifice of the
"unconscious" soldier is simultaneously a mutilation
of the *philosopheme* of representation. Turning now
toward the *montage* Bataille/Hegel, we would claim
that the exacerbation of the *Aufhebung*—or Hegelianism *sans réserve*—has the same structure as the
transition from the secondary ("normal") to the primary process: the flag—as the hysteria-bearing
object—"negates [*supprime*]" the fatherland in such a
manner that it is neither *conserved* nor *retained* by the
flag. Ruin of the *Aufhebung*/genesis of an unconscious . . .

But let us return to Marx. We have already linked
the extravagant expenditure(s) of Bonapartism to a
crisis of representation. But in that case, one is hard put
not to see in that frenetic circulation of money which
exhausts the fiscal policies of Bonaparte—Marx: "to
steal the whole of France in order to make a present of
her to France"—a Marxian counterpart to the ex-
tenuating circulation of meaning found in Freud (p.
206). This principle of absolute expenditure, in which
we would see an intuition of the utter mobility of
terms within a fantasmatic structure, is even apt to play
implicitly within Marx's theoretical formulations.
Such would be the case for the second paragraph of
The Eighteenth Brumaire, which begins with the well-
known statement: "Men make their own history, but
they do not make it as they please, under circumstances chosen by themselves; they do so under con-

ditions directly encountered, given, and transmitted from the past." The sentence may be read as a
precaution against a certain "spontaneist" humanism.
It posits the necessity of taking into account the historical constraints limiting every individual initiative.
And yet the paragraph, in concluding, sounds a quite
different note: "In like manner a beginner who has
learnt a new language always translates it back into his
mother tongue, but he has assimilated the spirit of the
new language and can freely express himself in it only
when he finds his way in it without recalling the old
and forgets his native tongue completely in the use of
the new." There is thus a movement in the paragraph
from an invocation of the ineluctable nature of history
as constraint to an active practice of forgetting. The
mother tongue is to be spent utterly in the exercise of
the second language: the Bonapartist move *par excellence* of repressing the ("constituent") mother. Such
would be the deviousness of "Bonapartism," escaping
Marx's analytic grasp, infiltrating the theoretical discourse of an author who can no longer quite write
about it.

1871: Shortly after the protracted massacre the French
term *la semaine sanglante,* Marx completed writing the
"Address of the General Council of the International
Working Men's Association on the Civil War in
France," a text we should note, whose illocutionary
force was quite different from those devoted to the
events of 1848–1852. For what was plainly at stake in
the later piece was mobilizing the sentiments provoked
by the events in Paris to political ends. We shall there-
fore not read the text as Marx's final statement on the

Commune. Indeed that last statement, in a letter of
1881 to Ferdinand Domela Nieuwenhuis, is rigorously
incompatible with the thesis of the Address: "You will
no doubt offer as an objection the case of the Paris
Commune, but aside from the fact that it was the in-
surrection of a single city in exceptional circumstances,
the majority of the Commune was by no means
socialist nor could it be . . . . "[23]

If we turn to the text on the Commune, it will be
rather to observe in it the insistence or repetition of the
structure we have delineated in the earlier works. That
structure, which informs the whole of Marx's analysis,
becomes manifest toward the end of the Address:
"That after the most tremendous war of modern
times, the conquering and the conquered host [Bis-
marck and Thiers] should fraternize for the common
massacre of the proletariat—this unparalleled event
indicates not, as Bismarck thinks, the final repression
of a new society upheaving, but the crumbling into
dust of *bourgeois* society. The highest heroic effort of
which the old society is still capable is national war;
and this is now proved to be a mere governmental
humbug, intended to defer the struggle of classes, and
to be thrown aside as soon as that class struggle bursts
into civil war . . . ." Worse yet: "Whenever before has
history exhibited the spectacle of a conqueror crowning his victory by turning into, not only the gendarme,
but the hired bravo of the conquered government?"[24]
Thus Marx approaches the Commune through a cer-

23. Quoted in Marx, *Sur la Commune de Paris* (Moscow: Editions
du progrès, 1971), p. 291.
24. "The Civil War in France" (New York: International Publishers, 1969), p. 68.

tain hilarity, however anxious, at the comedy that the
states of Europe seem to be playing out. But this comedy is none other than that of the panting contortions
of a dialectic of master (Bismarck) and slave (Thiers)
no longer able to dissimulate the profound servility of
the master (become hired thug or "bravo"). We should
note as well the extent of Marx's admiration for the
war and all the resources it is able to mobilize, "the
highest heroic effort of which the old society is still
capable . . ." For that admiration, no doubt, corres-
ponds to Marx's estimation of the Hegelian systematic, whose cornerstone, the dialectic of master and
slave, informs his perception of the war.

Thus the Commune which, according to Marx, was
a conflict "grafted" onto the national war, which
figures the excess of a dialectic *beside itself,* can be
superimposed, within the general economy of Marx's
work, on . . . the Bonapartist state. In order to gauge
the strangeness of this ruse, maneuver, or burrow of
the old mole, we need but note that for Jacques
Rougerie, France's premier historian of the Commune, Marx's "merveilleuse découverte" in the Address to the International was: "L'antithèse de l'Em-
pire, c'était la Commune."[25] To resolve or even elaborate the paradox is a task, we would suggest, worthy of
the "ideal laborer" invoked by Lacan in the epigraph to
this chapter. An initial observation, however: from its
inception, our reading has tended to regard the *register*
of antithesis as deceptive precisely to the extent that the
active fragment of the text was located in a dissymetry

25. "Karl Marx, l'Etat et la Commune" in *Preuves* (1968), No.
213, p. 46.

out of phase with every dualism. And this is even more
the case, as Rougerie himself seems inclined to admit,
for the somewhat sentimental antitheses of the 1871
text: "Paris all truth, Versailles all lie . . . ."[26]

Let us return, then, to the Commune in Marx's text,
or rather in the writings of those most successful in
exploiting certain implications of that text. First, Engels in the conclusion of his 1891 preface to Marx's
Address: "Of late, the Social-Democratic philistine
has once more been filled with wholesome terror at the
words: Dictatorship of the Proletariat. Well and good,
gentlemen, do you want to know what this dictatorship looks like? Look at the Paris Commune. That was
the Dictatorship of the Proletariat." For any understanding of how that dictatorship functions and stops
functioning, the crucial text is *Anti-Dühring*: "The first
act in which the state really comes forth as the representative of society as a whole—the taking possession
of the means of production in the name of society—is
at the same time its last independent act as a state. The
interference of the state power in social relations becomes superfluous in one sphere after another, and
then ceases of itself. The government of persons is
replaced by the administration of things and the direction of the processes of production. The state is not
'abolished,' *it fades away*."[27] Now, it is precisely this
model of a *withering away of the state* which informs
Lenin's reading of the Commune in *The State and Revolution*: "And once the majority of the people *itself*
suppresses its oppressors, a 'special force' for suppres-

26. "The Civil War in France," p. 68.
27. *Werke*, XX (Berlin: Dietz Verlag, 1968), p. 262.

sion *is no longer necessary*. In this sense, the state *begins to wither away*."[28] Thus Lenin—whose remarks here are inserted in a more general critique of specularity, i.e., of two antithetical ways, anarchist and opportunist, of misconstruing Marx's text—would see in the Commune the concrete form assumed by the withering away of the state. But it is precisely here that we may intuit the devious path joining "the Bonapartist state" and "the Commune," rendering them superimposable as the sites of a common heterogeneity in what 'we would call the Marxian fantasmatic. For "Bonapartism" in 1852 was shot through with a metaphorics of rot. The rotten or putrefying state, composed of the residues of class society, the *lumpen dejecta* of the class struggle, functioned as a source of rot within the theory as well. In 1871, Marx's text generates a Commune which is already potentially a *residue*-state, a simple vestige in the process of *decaying or withering away*, the way *out* of the class struggle. Our speculative conclusion? Between the putrefying or rotting state of 1852 and the decaying or withering state which, in 1871, *seems* so antithetically opposed to it, there transpires in Marx's text as devious a bit of dreamwork as that agency of the uncanny is capable of.

Finally, a telling parallel: at the very point at which academic Marxism rejects Marx's "Bonapartism" in its extreme manifestation, it seems to refuse as well the interpretation of the Commune as the withering away of the state. We have already seen M. Rubel find the Marxian break with representation "irrecevable." Here now is J. Rougerie on Engels' reading of the

28. Lenin, p. 50.

Commune: "Solution de l'entre-deux—mais est-elle pour autant synthétique?—et qui ôte, dans sa simplicité pratique, tout ce qu'il y avait de verdeur féroce dans l'exécration marxienne de l'Etat, dont Marx crédita les communards héroïques."[29] It is precisely that undecidable *entre-deux,* refractory to every synthesis, that Marx produced in the instances of "Bonapartism" (1852) and "the Commune" (1871), and it is in just such an *entre-deux* that we have situated our effort to delineate the multiple strands that bind them. Emblematically, in the distance: the *unheimlich* labors of the mole; the *untimely* collapse of the Vendôme column.

There would thus be inscribed within—or between—these texts of Marx, which are historico-political analyses, a strange theoretical novel. We are inclined to designate that theory "Freudian" to the extent that the fate of Marx's "Bonapartism" seems to repeat—or anticipate—the case, elaborated elsewhere, of Freud's "pleasure principle."[30] What we are faced with is a heterogeneous instance which is gradually assimilated by what initially seemed opposed to it in a manner far more asymmetrical than any evoked by the figure of antithesis. Or rather, that assimilation is nothing but the growing possibility, acquired by that instance, to be read as deriving its being from insertion in a specular and antithetical dualism: the Bonapartist slave (in 1870–1871) plays fallguy for his Prussian master in the comedy of dialectic. (Freud: the pleasure principle in 1920 moves into the conceptual orbit of

29. Rougerie, p. 54.
30. See Laplanche, *Vie et mort en psychanalyse.*

Eros, the bound and binding sexuality of narcissism.)
Whereupon a new version of that heterogeneity irrupts: Marx (Engels, Lenin), the Commune, the withering away of the state; Freud, the death instinct, the
destruction of the organism. We are, then, perhaps as
justified in terming the problematic Marxian as Freudian.

And yet there is a specifically psychoanalytic dimension to the process we have delineated in the texts of
Marx. I refer to the relation between the "theoretical"
and "political" strata of our analyses, and specifically
to the fact that the heterogeneous instance—in which
is condensed a maximum of "dreamwork," of "unconscious," of "the repressed"—should have elected
to cathect the term *State,* the repressive, or rather *sup-
pressive* agency *par excellence* for the political analysis.
For if, as we have suggested, what is *umheimlich* about
the *unheimlich* is that absolutely anything may be *unheimlich,* it is the impertinence or impropriety of that
anything that seems intended by the unconscious ca-
thexis of "the state." If the "Freudian" *effect* is always
located . . . where it shouldn't be—in this case in the
exteriority we may epitomize as "Marx"—the repressed presses its thoroughly indecent audacity to the
point of coinciding with the agency of suppression. It
is as though the texts, in their "Freudian" dimension,
affirmed, against every Marcusean accommodation,
the irreducibility of the category of repression (*Ver-
drängung*) to its more benign doublet, suppression (*Un-
terdruckung*). If there is indeed a *break* in these texts, it is
by no means between a truth and an ideology which
would have originally suppressed or masked it. It is

rather in the heterogeneous movement which would endlessly emancipate an *unheimlich* dimension indifferent to the distinctions: truth/error, suppressor/suppressed. To generate that *unheimlich* within *The Eighteenth Brumaire* and the texts through which it is ramified is tantamount to delineating the perverse rigor with which the repressed comes to identify with "Bonapartism" itself. The upshot: a Marx more profoundly an-archical than Anarchism ever dreamed, and an initial step taken toward the difficult articulation of Freud's text and the apparently *extrinsic* concerns of Marx.

II.

LITERATURE

> The Bonapartist dynasty represents not the en-
> lightenment, but the superstition of the peasant; not
> his judgment, but his prejudice; not his future, but his
> past; not his modern Cévennes, but his latter-day
> Vendée.   MARX, *The Eighteenth Brumaire*
> *of Louis Bonaparte*

There is an obvious impropriety in turning to the
works of Victor Hugo after a consideration of those of
Marx. Indeed Marx himself was the first to remind us
of the essential incompatibility of their enterprises. In
the preface to the second German edition of *The Eighteenth Brumaire* (1869), the author of *Napoléon-le-petit*
figures, along with Proudhon, as a fundamentally deluded commentator on the events of 1851: "Victor
Hugo confines himself to bitter and witty invective
against the responsible publisher of the *coup d'état*. The
event itself appears in his work like a bolt from the
blue. He sees in it only the violent act of a single individual . . . ."[1] Here we find the rudiments of a Marxian critique of Hugo's ideology in all the excess of its
individualist idealism. And indeed we might imagine

1. *Der Achtzehnte Brumaire des Louis Bonaparte* (Berlin: Dietz Verlag, 1972), p. 7.

just such a critique coming to saturate, with more or
less subtlety, an important segment of Hugo's *oeuvre*.
But our purpose in these pages will not be to offer that
demonstration (of a Marxian truth or theory of—
specifically Hugolian—literature), to reduce Hugo's
apparent error through a redeeming or rectifying *application* of Marxian categories. Rather shall we attempt to pursue our previously announced project of
delineating the refraction of the phenomenon of revolution in France through two divergent series of
writings: those of Marx, the subject of our previous
chapter, and, in the present one, in anticipation of other
nineteenth century novels, Hugo's *Quatrevingt-treize*.

The impropriety of juxtaposing Marx and Hugo,
the difference between the two series, is thus worth
keeping alive. For to work too rapid an alignment of
Marxian and literary categories, to imagine them re-
conciled in a Marxist theory of literature, would be to
blind us to a historical reality which more than any
other should serve as a touchstone for our inquiry. I
refer to the fierce and virtually unanimous opposition
with which the major writers of France reacted to the
Commune.[2] In the light of that resistance, one is inclined to speculate that the analytic task *par excellence*
would be to delineate the polemical field in which the
two series—Marxian and literary—would reveal the
intricacies of their *incompatibility*. In which case, the
project of constructing a Marxist theory of literature
might be shown to be the most conventional and mis-
guided of academic fantasies. . .

2. For an extensive dossier on the subject, see Paul Lidsky, *Les
Ecrivains contre la Commune* (Paris: Maspero, 1970).

Were one to choose a figure emblematic of the institution of literature in the French nineteenth century, it would undoubtedly be Victor Hugo. Or "Victor Hugo, hélàs," in Gide's classic formulation. Indeed, the most significant index of the centrality of Hugo is—beyond the longevity of his life, the prolificacy of his production—the degree to which he remains unreadable today, i.e., the degree to which our own modernity is definable in terms of a reaction against Hugo. The dossier is worth reviewing. Mallarmé, in a text we shall return to, dates the inception of our modernity ("Jugez le goût très moderne") with the death of Hugo in 1885.[3] For Valéry, the problem of every French poet from 1840 to 1890, was "faire autre chose que Hugo."[4] For Lautréamont, he was the "grande tête molle"[5]; for Char, "obèse auguste, c'est le grand réussi des insensés, ou inversement"; worse yet, "Barnum hâbleur . . . dans son entier il est impossible."[6] Even Nietzsche, in his anti-Wagnerian phase, was led to see in Wagner "the Victor Hugo of music."[7] Mallarmé, Lautréamont, Nietzsche, Char, Valéry: the writers who have been most instrumental in forging the language of modernity (i.e., of marginality, of

3. "Crise de vers" in *Oeuvres complètes* (Paris: Pléiade, 1945), p. 362.
4. "Situation de Baudelaire" in *Oeuvres,* I (Paris: Pléiade, 1957), pp. 598–604.
5. Letter of 12 March 1870 in *Oeuvres complètes* (Paris: Corti, 1958), p. 401.
6. *Recherche de la base et du sommet* (Paris: Gallimard, 1971), pp. 118–119.
7. *The Case of Wagner,* trans. W. Kaufman (New York: Vintage, 1967), p. 173.

fragmentation) invariably have defined themselves in opposition to the central presence of Hugo. Let that be sufficient grounds for the role in which he is here to be engaged: as metonym of Literature itself in the French nineteenth century.

Within Hugo's *oeuvre,* his principal treatment of re-volution is his final novel, *Quatrevingt-treize.* Indeed it may well be regarded as a work resonant with the entire history of ideological debate on revolution in the nineteenth century. For it is a novel written on the morrow of the Commune (1872–1873) about the Ter-ror of the Great Revolution by an author whose ideol-ogy, as late as 1872, was preeminently that of 1848. This last factor deserves comment, for in many ways it allows us to pinpoint Hugo's specificity within his cen-tury. From Lukacs to Barthes, that century has been interpreted as following a somewhat parabolic—or Icarian—trajectory, marked by the central tragedy of June 1848. Until that date the typical stance of the (*bourgeois*) writer was to criticize his class in the name of the values of his class: the more generous aspirations of the Enlightenment and of 1789. Thus Lamartine, for example, advocating a Girondist *bourgeoisie* in the face of the *bourgeoisie* of Louis-Philippe. With the traumatic massacres of 1848, however, the situation changes. Once the illusions of liberalism had been dispelled, the scenario goes, the writer in France could no longer appeal to the ideology of his class and came gradually, in the second half of the century, to regard his activity as a tactic in what Mallarmé referred to as his "strike [*grève*] against society."[8] It is against this backdrop that

8. *Oeuvres complètes,* p. 870.

the uniqueness of Hugo's stance is to be situated. For it was after the events of June that Hugo became a committed republican, a militant advocate of the values of February. The remarkable untimeliness of Hugo's move, which continues, I suspect, to account for his unreadability, is nicely captured in P. Albouy's paradoxical formula: "Hugo, en entrant dans l'histoire, tourne le dos à son temps."[9] To return to our principal focus, if Hugo is imaginable for the nineteenth century as Literature incarnate, that century enters the literature of Hugo with maximal density in his final novel *Quatrevingt-treize,* or 1793 judged in the light of (February) 1848 in the wake of 1871.

In order to facilitate our analysis, a skeletal outline of the novel's plot will prove helpful at this juncture. The action of *Quatrevingt-treize* is, for the most part, situated in the counter-revolutionary western region of the Vendée. The First Part of the book focuses on the clandestine maritime arrival of Lantenac, an aged but iron-willed aristocrat, onto the Breton shore. His purpose: to assume command of the Vendée counter-revolution and to pursue it mercilessly. The Second Part introduces us to Cimourdain, a former priest, a monster of austerity, who has joined the revolution and emerged as one of its most uncompromising Jacobin ideologues. Cimourdain accepts from the Committee of Public Safety a mission as *délégué civil* in the Vendée, charged specifically with assuring that any act of clemency on the part of the Republican army, any

9. Pierre Albouy, "Hugo fantôme" in *Littérature,* No. 13 (February 1974), p. 115.

failure to rout out the counter-revolution "without
grace," be punished with death. Finally, the third principal character, through whom the plot takes on its
tragic—or melodramatic—intensity: Gauvain. He is
the almost effeminately handsome young aristocrat,
who, out of sheer spontaneous generosity, has joined
the revolution and emerged as the commander of the
Republican army in the Vendée. In addition, Gauvain,
whose generosity has been known to lead him to acts
of clemency, has special ties to the two previously
mentioned characters. He is the detested great-nephew
of Lantenac. More important for the plot, he was
raised as a child by none other than Cimourdain,
whose sole—and overwhelming—affective invest-
ment in life, with the exception of the revolution, has
been his love for Gauvain. In brief, the novel pits
great-uncle and nephew against each other militarily,
and posits a potential conflict—over the question of
clemency—between Gauvain and his former preceptor. If tragedy there be, it will turn, unclassically, on
the question of pity midst Terror.

The events of the drama are mediated, however,
through the activities of a fourth (and entirely secondary) character, Michelle Fléchard, a peasant widow of
the Vendée, along with her three young children. She
is, for Hugo, a sublimely pre-political incarnation of
maternity, and the novel's action begins when she is
discovered—in terrified ignorance, hiding in the Vendée forest—by the revolutionary batallion of
Bonnet-Rouge, and then allowed to join the batallion,
which in turn adopts her three adored children. Eventually, just prior to Lantenac's assumption of control

over the counter-revolution, the batallion of Bonnet-Rouge is defeated by the "blancs," and Lantenac orders that all but the children be slaughtered. The children are taken (potentially hostage) by Lantenac's forces. Michelle Fléchard, however, left for dead, eventually revives and will devote the rest of her efforts to recovering her children.

In the final—and longest—section of the novel (Part III), Lantenac and his diminished forces, the last hope of the Vendée, are besieged in the massive defensive tower of the Gauvain castle (La Tourgue). The children, virtual mascots of the Revolution, are being held hostage, locked in a library adjoining the tower. Lantenac's threat: unless Gauvain allows him freedom to leave, the library will be set aflame and the children will perish by fire. In the deluded expectation that he will nevertheless be able to save the children, Gauvain refuses the counter-revolutionary bargain and begins the attack. The battle begins; the library is set aflame; the rescue ladder fails to arrive; and Lantenac, improbably, discovers a secret underground passage that allows him to escape La Tourgue. At this point, a haggard Michelle Fléchard staggers onto the surrounding plane and, realizing that her children are in the burning library, emits a shriek of maternal grief that has a transfiguring effect on Lantenac, still in the vicinity of the castle. He alone has the key to the iron door of the library; he returns to the castle and, at the risk of his life, saves the children. Greeted by a grateful "Vive la république!," he responds scornfully, "Vive le roi!" He is taken prisoner.

At this point, Gauvain's moral dilemma becomes

the focus of Hugo's attention. Convinced that the revolution *he* has championed cannot choose to punish
an act of self-sacrifice of the magnitude of Lantenac's,
he enters Lantenac's prison cell and, after being scornfully insulted by his great-uncle, throws his military
cloak over Lantenac's shoulders and casts him
out . . . to his freedom. The following day Cimourdain finds himself forced to officiate at the court-
martial of . . . Gauvain, the one person in the world he
loves. He casts the deciding vote against Gauvain.
Gauvain's final words before being guillotined are:
"Vive la République!" Cimourdain, at the very moment the guillotine takes Gauvain's life, shoots himself
fatally in the heart. The novel ends with an evocation
of some celestial reunion of the two "sister souls."

Were we to attempt to unify the baroque prolifera-
tions of Hugo's plot around a single thematic motif, it
might well be what G. Rosa, in as shrewd an analysis as
the novel has received, terms "la double appartenance."[10] For the moments of maximum intensity in
Quatrevingt-treize are those in which a character finds
himself the locus of two conflicting sets of norms.
Thus, Lantenac, at the turning point of the novel, must
choose between his potential commitment to the
counter-revolution and the "pre-political" moral
claim which the situation of the three menaced children makes on him. Similarly, Gauvain, before rescu-
ing Lantenac, is caught in debate between the terroris-
tic claims of the Revolution and the more generous

10. Guy Rosa, "Présentation de *Quatrevingt-treize*" in Hugo,
Oeuvres complètes, Vol. XV, ed. Jean Massin (Paris: Club français
du livre, 1970), p. 235.

aspirations of his ideal Republic: "La Terreur com-
promet la République et sauve la Révolution."[11] If the
novel is about revolution, revolution *for Hugo* is an
essentially moral affair. Its precondition is an individual trapped between conflicting duties; its realization,
the individual's decision to choose against his self-
interest. And to the extent that Hugo obscurely intuited that self-interest is essentially class interest, we
may summarize Hugo's characteristically un-Marxian
stance, along with Rosa, as follows: "L'appartenance
de classe n'est constitutive de la progression historique
que pour autant qu'on la nie."[12]

The beginning of Revolution for Hugo is thus the
possibility of class betrayal. Whence, for example, the
understandable disapproval of Lukacs: "The real,
human and historical collisions of the aristocrat and the
priest, who have allied themselves with the Revolution, are turned into ingenious conflicts of duty based
on (an) abstract humanism."[13] But what we would
insist on in the present context is less the degree of
"realism" in Hugo's portrayal of the Terror than on
the essential impossibility which structures his vision
of revolution. For a relentlessness in working against
one's own interest is ultimately suicidal. And it is in
this light that the various suicidal decisions (Lantenac,
Gauvain, Cimourdain) affirmed by Hugo in the culmination of the novel together manifest a certain bankruptcy of his political thought. The emblematic situa-

11. Cited from "Reliquat de *Quatrevingt-treize*" in Rosa, p. 245.
12. Rosa, p. 238.
13. G. Lukacs, *The Historical Novel,* trans. H. and S. Mitchell,
(London: Penguin, 1962), p. 308.

tion here is Gauvain presenting to Cimourdain what is essentially Hugo's philosophy of revolution in prison, just prior to his execution. The political program is issued at a time when its impotence is most glaring. Whence, moreover, the angelic, otherworldly character of Gauvain. Class betrayal, the beginning of revolution, would seem as well, in every sense of the word, the *end* of revolution.

How might one interpret the viciously circular impasse which structures the novel? Rosa's answer is an appeal to the Sartre of *Qu'est-ce que la littérature?*. In the eighteenth century, according to Sartre, the freedoms requisite for the practice of literature were indistinguishable from the political liberties sought by the citizenry: "il suffit à l'écrivain d'explorer l'arbitraire de son art et de se faire l'interprète de ses exigences formelles pour devenir révolutionnaire."[14] By the second half of the following century, the situation had changed considerably. The political impotence of literature resulted in—or was manifest as—three aberrant tendencies: simple acceptance of the values of the newly successful oppressive class; a refusal of the *bourgeois* public in the form of the calculated aggressions of *l'art pour l'art*; the search for a new mass audience, dubbed *le Peuple*. Hugo's choice was, of course, the third, but it was shot through with contradiction. For the appeal to the People took the form of an abstract humanitarianism which was nothing but the ideology *par excellence* of the *bourgeoisie*. If the class particularity of the *bourgeoisie* is to pretend to incarnate "universal values," the more the *bourgeois* writer

14. *Qu'est-ce que la littérature?* (Paris: Gallimard, 1948), p. 164.

would venture to affirm positions beyond class the
more would the classbound character of his enterprise
be apparent. The structure of the predicament of the
bourgeois writer in search of a mass public in the late
nineteenth century is viciously circular in the manner
of what Sartre calls elsewhere a "non-synthetic
unification."[15] Or of the endeavors of the heroes of
Quatrevingt-treize, relentlessly bent on choosing
against their own interest. For if one reads the novel as
an affirmation of an unrestrained will to failure; and if
one is radical in adopting its political-ethical program,
then one will always fail to the extent that one succeeds
in its pursuit, and succeed to the extent that one fails.
Hugo's dilemma as a writer would engage him in a
project ultimately as self-defeating as those of the
characters in *Quatrevingt-treize,* and the philosophico-
analytical model of their joint predicament would be
the "whirligig [*tourniquet*]," the viciously circular construct which has been the elective object of the critical
efforts of Jean-Paul Sartre.

   Perhaps. Sartre in *Les Mots,* after all, has defined his
life's work as a frenetic critique of "Victor Hugo." For
Karl Schweitzer, the cultural model of his youth, like
many men of his era, like Victor Hugo himself, we are
told, took himself for Victor Hugo: Jean-Paul Sartre,
then, or the mad passion to dismantle the exemplary
illusions of Victor Hugo. Our reading of *Quatrevingt-
treize* thus begins with that stratum of the work available to a Sartrian reading. And yet Rosa's (Sartrian)
interpretation may prove even more valuable to us in

   15. For a discussion of "non-synthetic unification" in Sartre, see
my *Structural Study of Autobiography: Proust, Leiris, Sartre, Lévi-
Strauss* (Ithaca: Cornell, 1974), pp. 174–186.

our present attempt to draw Hugo's novel *out* of the vicious circle through two crucial lapses in its argument. To these we now turn.

The first concerns Rosa's reading of the Vendée. For Hugo's book is pre-eminently a "novel of the Vendée," and one's interpretation of that phrase bears important consequences for one's global comprehension of the work. For Rosa, the Vendée offers the spectacle *par excellence* of a struggle against one's own interests: "Le paradoxe ici n'est que dans la violence d'une lutte qui oppose les libérés à leurs libérateurs."[16] The exemplary configuration—the *tourniquet*—is at work here, and one might even maintain that the peasant counter-revolutionaries are, from Hugo's point of view, virtually "revolutionary" in the catastrophic *dis*-interest with which they fight. And yet to read Hugo on the Vendée is to encounter a dimension far too anarchical to be subsumed by even the kind of viciously circular project thematized by Sartre: "La Bretagne est une vieille rebelle. Toutes les fois qu'elle s'était révoltée pendant deux mille ans, elle avait eu raison; la dernière fois, elle a eu tort. Et pourtant au fond, contre la révolution comme contre la monarchie, contre les représentants en mission comme contre les gouverneurs ducs et pairs, contre la planche aux assignats comme contre la ferme des gabelles . . . c'était toujours la même guerre que la Bretagne faisait, la guerre de l'esprit local contre l'esprit central" (p. 396).[17] It is as though the opposition revolution/counter-revolution were too symmetrical, too indif-

16. Rosa, p. 238.
17. Page references in the text are to vol. XV of Hugo, *Oeuvres complètes,* ed. Jean Massin (Paris: Club français du livre, 1970).

ferently *centered* on the prerogatives of the capital to
embrace a reality that exceeded it in a crucial way:
"Toutes les fois que le centre, Paris, donne une impulsion, que cette impulsion vienne de la royauté ou de la
république, qu'elle soit dans le sens du despotisme ou
dans le sens de la liberté, c'est une nouveauté, et la
Bretagne se hérisse" (p. 396). The Vendée is thus the
name given to a region compulsively resistent to every
attempt at centralization (or totalization): monar-
chical, republican, or, dare we say, Sartrian. For the
dogged refusal of the Vendée to entertain that min-
imal degree of (centralizing) organization that would
allow for the identification of one's interest effectively
shatters any effort to comprehend the region *within* the
category of project.

Spiritually and linguistically the Vendée is a kind of
wound within the mind of France: "parlant une langue
morte, ce qui est faire habiter une tombe à sa pensée"
(p. 388). And the silence of that tomb comes to
epitomize the region itself, thus characterized in a
paragraph two words in length: "Surdité terrible."
But that silence affects as well an additional form of
communication, the subterranean network through
which the peasants pursue their guerilla activities:
"cette vie souterraine était immémoriale en Bretagne"
(p. 389). "Le sous-sol de telle forêt était une sorte de
madrépore percé et traversé en tous sens par une voirie
inconnue de sapes, de cellules et de galeries." (p. 390)
To describe the Vendée would be to chart a multilinear
system of underground tunnels reminiscent for Hugo
of Egypt: "Voilà ce que Cambyse trouva en Egypte et
ce que Westermann trouva en Bretagne" (p. 389). For
Hugo, life in Brittany is, in every sense, *low*: "La Ven-

dée a avorté. D'autres révoltes ont réussi, la Suisse
par exemple. Il y a cette différence entre l'insurgé
de montagne comme le Suisse et l'insurgé de forêt
comme le Vendéen, que, presque toujours, fatale
influence du milieu, l'un se bat pour un idéal, et l'autre
pour des préjugés. L'un plane, l'autre rampe . . . l'un
est sur une cime, l'autre est dans une ombre . . . .
L'éducation n'est point la même, faite par les sommets,
ou par les bas-fonds" (p. 395). The antitheses here
are those of Bataille's anti–surrealist text: *"La vieille
taupe et le préfixe sur dans les mots surhomme et surréalisme."* [18] Breton, it may be recalled, referred to Victor
Hugo as "surréaliste quand il n'était pas bête." [19]
Bataille scorned Hugo for casting his lot with the
suraigles, and sought to affirm a specific mode of *bêtise.*
But for Hugo, to write a novel of the Vendée would
inevitably be to affirm just such a relation to lowness.
As for the "beast": the counter–revolutionaries act as
jaguars "ayant des moeurs de *taupes*" (p. 390).

A second lapse in Rosa's analysis. In an effort to
demonstrate how the ethical scheme of "double appartenance" has priority over the depiction of character in the novel, the critic states that at its most intense
the dilemma *within* each character may be viewed as
the impossible point of intersection between the values
of that character and those of another one. And to that
extent: "chaque personnage est le manque d'un autre." [20] Thus, at the turning point of the novel Lantenac's choice pits his royalist rigor against values

18. *Oeuvres complètes,* Vol. II, (Paris: Gallimard, 1970), pp. 93–
109.
19. *Les Manifestes du surréalisme* (Paris: Le Sagittaire, 1955), p. 25.
20. Rosa, p. 249.

which we have come to associate with Gauvain. And
Gauvain's inner debate opposes his own generous in-
clinations to imperatives issuing from Cimourdain
which he shares equally. But what of Cimourdain's
decision at the novel's end? Rosa: "En se suicidant,
Cimourdain reconnaît qu'il ne peut ni désavouer ses
propres idées ni les garder. Il se condamne au nom de
ses propres principes pour avoir adopté ceux de Gauvain, ou au nom de ceux de Gauvain pour avoir con-
servé les siens."[21] And yet there is no evidence that
Cimourdain ever comes to share Gauvain's views.
Our sense is rather that his suicide is dictated by sheer
grief at his assumed responsibility for the death of the
one creature he has loved. Let us, moreover, recall the
quality of his affection. Early in the novel we are told:
"L'esprit allaite; l'intelligence est une mamelle. Il y a
analogie entre la nourrice qui donne son lait et le pré-
cepteur qui donne sa pensée" (p. 349). At the novel's
end, Cimourdain slips into Gauvain's cell and observes
him asleep: "Une mère regardant son nourrisson dor-
mir n'aurait pas un plus tendre et plus inexprimable
regard" (p. 501). The character of Cimourdain's grief
is thus maternal. A pressure in the text leads Hugo
twice to imagine the preceptor as having mothered the
young hero.

   To touch on the theme of maternity in *Quatrevingt-
treize* is, of course, to engage a central theme of the
novel, and perhaps even the theme of—or as—the
very dimension of centrality. For the work begins with
a theatrical *tableau* in which the soldiers of the republican batallion encircle what they suspect to be their

21. *Ibid.*, p. 245.

enemy only to find they have surrounded a helpless mother, Michelle Fléchard, and her three infants. More important still, the turning point of the novel is the sheer bestial cry of Michelle at the sight of her children in the flaming library: "La mère reconnut ses enfants. Elle jeta un cri effrayant. Ce cri de l'inexprimable angoisse n'est donné qu'aux mères. Rien n'est plus farouche, et rien n'est plus touchant" (p. 475). It is Michelle's shriek that works the transfiguring effect on Lantenac. The cry then, in all its phonic presence, is the voice of nature itself, nature—or maternity—as voice, an irreducible reality beyond which, Hugo would seem to be saying, one cannot go.[22] The novel thus affirms the grounding—and central—function of voice, a particularly appropriate development in a work as blatantly "operatic" as *Quatrevingt-treize*.[23]

What then are the results of our examination of two acts of misreading in Rosa's (Sartrian) analysis of the

22. This valorization of voice, however pre-political its pretensions in the case of *Quatrevingt-treize,* was an important element in Hugo's politics. Thus in *Napoléon-le-Petit,* the Revolution (of 1789) is incarnate in the oratory of the Tribune, "le lieu le plus sonore du monde" (*Oeuvres complètes,* vol. VIII, p. 487). "De cette tribune sans cesse en vibration, partaient perpétuellement des sortes d'ondes sonores, d'immenses oscillations de sentiments et d'idées qui, de flot en flot et de peuple en peuple, allaient aux confins de la terre remuer ces vagues intelligentes qu'on appelle des âmes . . . " (p. 488).

23. In the Paris section of the novel, one comes across what seems almost a stage direction for the duet of insults between Marat and Robespierre: "Ils continuèrent sur un ton de causerie dont la lenteur accentuait la violence des répliques et des ripostes, et ajoutait on ne sait quelle ironie à la menace" (p. 358). One is hard put not to imagine the whole scene set to music by Verdi.

novel? The first case, once read, has put us in closer contact with the Vendée as *scene* of the text: a silent, subterranean network, "partial [*partielle*]" in its essence, resistant to every effort at centralization. The second lapse entailed a failure—or refusal—to recognize the specifically *maternal* quality of Cimourdain's grief. But to broach the subject of maternity was quickly to move to the pivotal point of the novel, in which maternity, reduced to its *vocal* essence, comes to determine the future course of the action. There is, then, a significant relation between the two errors we have focused on. We would suggest that the novel the Sartrian refused to read was, at some level, concerned with the primal power of voice dictating the action of a drama set against a plurilinear and mute—or deaf— backdrop of . . . what? Let us not yet answer that question, which shall be the implicit concern orienting the analyses to follow. We shall simply note at this juncture the oddity of positing a dimension (our mute "backdrop") *behind* the primal. For is not primacy that reality beyond or behind which one cannot think? That question as well shall occupy us in the ensuing reading.

We are confronted, then, with what might be termed the proto-text of *Quatrevingt-treize,* a construct so bare that it is reducible to an inaugural blast of sound in a ramifying field of deafness, an elaboration so tenuous that it may be defined as nothing else than what was *missed* by a particularly strong (Sartrian) reading of the novel. For that reason we are drawn to observe that in a chapter of the book, tellingly entitled "Aures habet, et non audiet," Hugo presents, in the form of an episode, a process homologous in structure to that of our "proto-text." Lantenac, arriving exhausted on the Breton beach, savoring the silence and desolation of the spot, is suddenly distracted by a strange and distant sight, the church tower of Cormeray:

> La silhouette de ce clocher se découpait nettement; on voyait la tour surmontée de la pyramide, et, entre la tour et la pyramide, la cage de la cloche, carrée, à jour, sans abat-vent, et ouverte aux regards des quatre côtés, ce qui est la mode des clochers bretons.
>
> Or cette cage apparaissait alternativement ouverte et fermée, à intervalles égaux; sa haute fenêtre se dessinait toute blanche, puis toute noire; on voyait le ciel à travers, puis on ne le voyait plus; il y avait clarté, puis occultation, et l'ouverture et la fermeture se succédaient d'une seconde à l'autre avec la régularité du marteau sur l'enclume. (p. 325)

Lantenac observes the same odd alternation of black and white in a series of church towers proliferating on the horizon. He pauses in wonderment and soon comes to grasp the import of his observations:

> On sonnait le tocsin, on le sonnait frénétiquement, on le sonnait partout, dans tous les clochers, dans toutes les paroisses, dans tous les villages, et l'on n'entendait rien.
>
> Cela tenait à la distance qui empêchait les sons d'arriver et au vent de mer qui soufflait du côté opposé et qui emportait tous les bruits de la terre hors de l'horizon.
>
> Toutes ces cloches forcenées, appelant de toutes parts, et en même temps ce silence, rien de plus sinistre.
>
> Le vieillard regardait et écoutait.
>
> Il n'entendait pas le tocsin, et il le voyait. Voir le tocsin, sensation étrange. (p. 325)

In the following chapter, Lantenac is apprised for whom the bell tolls: for himself. What we are presented with, then, is a bizarre differential movement generating the most present and identificatory of sounds. The alternation of light and dark is prior to the subsequent induction of sound just as the plurilinear deafness of the Vendée is located *behind* the primacy of voice. Or rather, what the chapter under consideration presents in time our proto-text posits in space, unless, of course, the differential process involved is disruptive of the distinction time/space even as it plays havoc with the opposition between part (chapter) and whole (novel). In each case the ramifying pre-acoustic dimension is invested with an Egyptian motif: the *pyramid* shaped top of the tower; the analogy between the underground networks in Brittany and in the ancient monarchy on the Nile. In view of the perverse rigor with which the two moments mesh, one begins to wonder whether the apparently minor episode of "Aures habet" is not in communication with larger issues in the novel, and, more immediately, with other episodes. More specifically, the hammer (*marteau*) and anvil (*enclume*) are metaphors for both the differential mechanism which silently produces sound and components of the ear. What message is being both received and disarticulated by that ear—and from where?

Before answering that question, we should pause to consider the stakes. If one could choose a single emblem of Hugo's unreadability it would be the prophetic bombast which led him to cast himself as beacon to humanity. Thus already Nietzsche: "Victor Hugo or the lighthouse on the sea of bilge [*der Pharus am Meere des Unsinns*]."[24] Consider now our proliferat-

24. Quoted in J. Maurel, "Hugo-Nietzsche: Métaphore impossible" in *Nietzsche aujourd'hui?*, II (Paris: 10/18, 1973), p. 61.

ing and silent *tocsin,* the towers by the sea with their perpetual eclipse and reappearance of light. The two towers—light house and bell-tower—seem versions of each other. Which is to suggest that there might be grounds for reinscribing the image of the lighthouse, reading it not in terms of a blinding and inflationary superabundance of light, but rather of a certain insufficiency of—and in—sound. At that point the "sunspots [*taches de soleil*]"—Valéry's condescending description of Hugo's failings—might grow, achieve parity with the source of light they block and, in a silent movement of alternation, proceed to undermine that cult of the grounding virtue of voice, and of the acoustic generally, which, in *Quatrevingt-treize,* is the privileged medium of Hugo's idealism.[25]

Nothing could be more "uncanny [*sinistre*]," Hugo tells us, than Lantenac's experience of the silent *tocsin.* And yet our reaction is one of even greater uncanniness at the realization that an identical process is at work within—and against—the turning point of the novel. After the bell-tower, La Tourgue, the fortress approached by Michelle in desperation as the battle begins:

> On eut dit que c'était la tour elle-même qui saignait et que la géante était blessée.
> Chose surprenante, cela ne faisait presque pas de bruit dehors. La nuit était très noire, et dans la plaine et dans la forêt il y avait autour de la forteresse attaquée une sorte de paix funèbre. Dedans c'était l'enfer, dehors c'était le

25. Valéry, *Oeuvres,* I, p. 586: "On peut bien trouver dans son oeuvre quantité de faiblesses et de taches, et memes d'énormes. Ce ne sont, grâce au magnifique reste, que les taches d'un soleil."

sépulcre. Ce choc d'hommes s'exterminant dans les
ténèbres, ces mousqueteries, ces clameurs, ces rages, tout ce
tumulte expirait sous la masse des murs et des voûtes, l'air
manquait au bruit, et au carnage s'ajoutait l'étouffement.
Hors de la tour, cela s'entendait à peine . . . . (p. 459)

With the defensive tower, as with the bell-tower, we
are impressed with the degree to which a prodigious
amount of sound is manifest above all as . . . silence. If
La Tourgue is silent, however, it is pre-eminently visible to the distressed mother as she arrives on the surrounding plain, and its visibility is marked by a specific
rhythm: "Les détonations étouffés et les lueurs pâles
qui sortaient de la tour avaient . . . des intermittences;
elles s'interrompaient, puis reprenaient, proposant on
ne sait quelle poignante énigme à la misérable mère en
détresse" (p. 473). Hugo continues: "cette flamme
apparaissait, puis disparaissait, avec ces torsions
farouches qu'ont les éclairs et les serpents. Cette
flamme sortait comme une langue de quelque chose
qui ressemblait à une gueule et qui était une fenêtre
pleine de feu" (p. 474). Shortly thereafter the mother
recognizes her children trapped in the library: "Elle
jeta un cri effrayant" (p. 475). Consider how oddly,
how mutely the present episode *speaks* (through its
langue, gueule) to the (ear—*marteau, enclume*—of the)
earlier one. In each case we find a prodigious absence of
sound manifest as an alternating visible rhythm, and
resulting, after the fact, in an acoustic experience so
intense as to be posited as the dimension of primacy
itself. Lantenac is struck to the quick by his eventual
realization of the purpose of the tocsin, just as he will

be devastated and transfigured by Michelle's shattering cry. But in each case that originary sound is de-
ferred, generated by a silent and repetitive play of difference. It is as though the circuit of self-presence or
interiority, whereby the "mouth" of the present
episode might commune—in the fulness of the
Logos—with the "ear" of the earlier one, were disrupted by the very movement which called it into *being*. Consider how different our two episodes are, how
gross a *category error* is entailed by our superimposition.
To claim that the differential movement of the tocsin
"results" in the sound of the bell just as the alternation
of the flames "results" in the cry of Michelle is to make
short shrift of the philosophically crucial distinction
between mechanical and motivational causality. Yet
the odd precision of the superimposition strikes me as
such as to lead one to posit a stratum of Hugo's text
weirdly subversive of such distinctions, to imagine a
mode of textual analysis thinkable as nothing so much
as the rigorous exploitation of category errors.

After the novel's turning point, we turn to its conclusion. For here again we encounter an oddly alternating mechanism in the form of the epitome of 1793, the
guillotine. It is an excrescence of lowness itself: "Il
semblait que cela était sorti de terre. Et cela en était
sorti en effet. Dans la terre fatale avait germé l'arbre
sinistre" (p. 506). And at the novel's end the Egyptian
reference serves to identify the differential apparatus as
a form of writing: "De loin sur l'horizon c'était une
silhouette faite de lignes droites et dures ayant l'aspect
d'une lettre hébraïque ou d'un de ces hiéroglyphes
d'Egypte qui faisaient partie de l'alphabet de l'antique

énigme" (p. 505). The writing machine, irredeemably
low, is also caught up in a process of substitution as
error, for the guillotine arrives on the scene of the
novel in place of the expected ladder awaited in order
to save the children. Our writing machine, in this case,
is offensively loud: the transfiguring execution of
Gauvain is perceived as a "coup hideux." And yet it
too serves as a generator of a certain silence. Consider
the timing of Cimourdain's suicide: "Au même instant
on en entendit un autre. Au coup de hache répondit un
coup de pistolet" (p. 509). To the extent that the second
"blow," the pistol shot, was simultaneous with the
first, it would pass undistinguished, essentially unheard. Once more the differential apparatus inscribes a
certain silence within a shattering sound. With what
result?: "Et ces deux âmes, soeurs tragiques, s'envol-
èrent ensemble, l'ombre de l'une mêlée à la lumière de
l'autre" (p. 509). The end is an idealizing flight of what
can only be construed, in view of our comments
above, as a hallucination of maternal *communion*. The
move toward the heights, occurring midst the ear-
splitting double *coup*, is thus congruent with the other
elements in our "phonic" series: the sound of the tocsin, the cry of Michelle. But we are now better placed
to judge the precise character of the alternating
machine which generates the dimension of acoustic
primacy even as it disarticulates it. For it is the bizarre
and almost dream-like movement of a hieroglyphic,
a form of script no longer subservient to the ideality
of voice. A writing machine, then, is what rips the
"tongue [*langue*]" of fire out of it *gueule* in the earlier
episode, prevents it from communing with the "ham-

mer" and "anvil" of "Aures habet," indeed destroys that very dimension of self-presence requisite for the formulation of any project. Whence the appropriateness of our proto-text, the infinitely tenuous *residue* of Rosa's Sartrian reading, generated as nothing more than what was *missed* by the categories of project: an almost incorporeal voice affirming its primacy against the ramifying field of plurilinear . . . script which embraces it. Recalling precisely the maternal function fulfilled by Cimourdain ("l'esprit allaite"), we may summarize metonymically the progress of our analysis: it is the silent and sinister alternation of the *tocsin* that generates the hysterical maternity—or *sein en toc*—of Cimourdain. Has our reading, then, the structure of a (bad) joke? Such was the embarrassed complaint addressed to Freud by the first readers of *Die Traumdeutung*; and such as well the observation that led him to write *Der Witz.* Let that example serve to encourage us. But Hugo himself, in *Les Misérables,* offers the right response here: "Le calembour est la fiente de l'esprit qui vole."[26] Flight and dung; idealism and its residue; the self-presence of the *logos* and writing. Our analysis—even in its humorous summary —has been deliberately *low.* It has attempted to coincide with that level of the text in which a general economy of writing comes to inscribe within it the hallucinated ideality of a voice. Our reading has been treacherous as well. For it would imply that in some sense the author of *Le Dernier jour d'un condamné,* the life-long polemicist against capital punishment, was

26. *Oeuvres complètes,* vol. X, p. 144.

affirming, in the form of the hieroglyph at the end of *Quatrevingt-treize,* the guillotine itself. *Itself?* As we have seen the writing machine repeat itself differently as tocsin, Tourgue, guillotine, and, in the proto-text, Vendée, we may be inclined to posit that just such a process is incompatible with the notion of identity, disruptive of every pretension to thematic presence. Our analysis, then: treacherous, like the Vendée; low, like the *taupe.* [27]

Interpretation as a sneak attack. On La Tourgue. For if the *book* may be regarded as a series of inhibiting defenses to be overcome, has not Hugo, in his description of the medieval fortress, given us a clue as to how to proceed? More specifically, we would suggest that the writing machine is in *Quatrevingt-treize* as the library is within the fortress, or as the Vendée is within France. For the library is virtually an internal enemy within the fortress. Within? In fact, it adjoins the defensive structure and is located in a bridge to the surrounding plain constructed in the seventeenth century: "Simplifiée à ce point, cette forteresse était, au moyen âge, à peu près imprenable. Le pont l'affaiblissait . . ." (p. 423). "Au point de vue militaire, le pont, insistons-y, livrait presque la tour. Il l'embellissait et la désarmait; en gagnant de l'ornement elle avait perdu de la force . . . . La bibliothèque et le grenier étaient pour l'assiégeant, et

27. In this excremental context, we are tempted to summarize J. Maurel's outrageous discourse on "Hugo-Nietzsche" at the 1972 Cerisy colloquium on Nietzsche (see footnote 24 above) as follows: Hugo is so full of shit, it so oozes from his every orifice, that he may indeed be Literature's first materialist.

contre la forteresse . . . ." (p. 424) The library-bridge
is thus neither within nor without La Tourgue. It is a
supplementary construct whose excess can be thematized only as a lack. In its very inception it is cut
off from its origin, a mere imitation: "Copier Versailles remplaça ceci: continuer les aïeux" (p. 423). And at
its center is an object whose authenticity is cast into
doubt:

> Il y avait dans cette bibliothèque des livres quelconques. Un
> est resté célèbre. C'était un vieil in-quarto avec estampes,
> portant pour titre en grosses lettres *Saint-Barthélémy*, et pour
> sous-titre *Evangile selon Saint Barthélémy, précédé d'une disser-*
> *tation de Pantoenus, philosophe chrétien, sur la question de savoir*
> *si cet évangile doit être réputé apocryphe et si Saint Barthélémy est*
> *le même que Nathanaël.* Ce livre, considéré comme
> exemplaire unique, était sur un pupitre au milieu de la bi-
> bliothèque" (p. 425)

Once again, the adjunct—or preface—marks the point
of vulnerability. The apocryphal *Saint-Barthélémy* in
the library is an image of the imitative library-bridge in
the fortress.

   For that reason we would draw attention to some of
the most intense writing in the novel, contained in the
section ("Livre troisième") entitled "Le Massacre de
Saint-Barthélémy." The events described in these pas-
sages are virtually simultaneous with the battle of La
Tourgue. They follow a somewhat depressingly sentimental celebration—by the author of *L'Art d'être*
grand-pere—of the three captive children and concern
Saint-Barthélémy: "Ce livre était beau; c'est pourquoi
René-Jean le regardait, trop peut-être. Le volume était
précisément ouvert à une grande estampe représentant

saint Barthélémy portant sa peau sur son bras . . . ."
His sister exclaims "Gimage," and René-Jean decides
to act on his "amour terrible" for the book:

> Puis quand la chaise toucha le pupitre, il monta dessus et
> posa ses deux poings sur le livre.
>
> Parvenu à ce sommet, il sentit le besoin d'être magnifique;
> il prit la "gimage" par le coin d'en haut et la déchira soig-
> neusement; cette déchirure de saint Barthélémy se fit de
> travers, mais ce ne fut pas la faute de René-Jean; il laissa dans
> le livre tout le côté gauche avec un oeil et un peu de l'auréole
> du vieil évangéliste apocryphe, et offrit à Georgette l'autre
> moitié du saint et toute sa peau. (p. 440)

The laceration of the "saint" proceeds meticulously,
page by page, until it reaches a turning point:

> Cela fait il [René-Jean] jeta le livre à terre.
> Ce fut un moment effrayant. Gros-Alain et Georgette
> virent, avec une extase mêlée d'épouvante, René-Jean
> froncer ses sourcils, roidir ses jarrets, crisper ses points et
> pousser hors du lutrin l'in-quarto massif. Un bouquin
> majesteux qui perd contenance, c'est tragique. Le lourd vol-
> ume désarçonné pendit un moment, hésita, se balança, puis
> s'écroula, et rompu, froissé, lacéré, déboîté dans sa reliure,
> disloqué dans ses fermoirs, s'aplatit lamentablement sur le
> plancher. (p. 441)

Soon the frenzy reaches a Dionysian pitch:

> René-Jean se précipita, Gros-Alain se rua, et joyeux, éper-
> dus, triomphants, impitoyables, déchirant les estampes,
> balafrant les feuillets, arrachant les signets, égratignant la
> reliure, décollant le cuir doré, déclouant les clous des coins
> d'argent, cassant le parchemin, déchiquetant le texte au-
> guste, travaillant des pieds, des mains, des ongles, des dents,
> roses, riants, féroces, les trois anges de proie s'abattirent sur
> l'évangeliste sans défense. (p. 441)

With just such ferocity and exhilaration is the book *par excellence,* and perhaps the institution of the book itself, dismantled in *Quatrevingt-treize*. And what are we to make of the fact that the destruction of a volume visible to us through its engraving of the martyrdom of Saint Bartholomew should be entitled the "massacre of Saint Bartholomew"? Is the suggestion not that the very subject or mode of existence of the volume is self-consumption, a radical bursting of its own binding? La Tourgue, then, can be *taken* through that site within it in which a book may be seen to be destroying itself. Just so have we attempted to *take Quatrevingt-treize,* by seizing on a writing machine perpetually different from itself as it moves from tocsin to Tourgue to guillotine, a differential apparatus that disarticulates the phonic plenitude orienting the novel's action and figures the instance whereby the book escapes from itself.

Escapes where? The question concerns the powers of the "machine" we have constructed. For we would suggest that a reading of a text be valued above all in terms of its capacity to "read" other texts, to liberate energies otherwise *contained* elsewhere. Moreover, to the extent that a reading would be radical, the quality of that energy should be determinable as a multiplicity of entirely *local* surprises. For there is a micropolitics of interpretation calculable in terms of effects that more teleologically oriented efforts—the very category "Marxist-theory-of-literature" is exemplary here—invariably miss. The most recent and impressive effort at such a theory is Julia Kristeva's *La Révolution du langage poétique,* 620 prodigiously intelligent pages in the service of a thesis so conventional as to be a commonplace of the West's most strident *avant-garde:* Mallarmé and Lautréamont seen as the major figures in an intra-literary process of "subversion" *analogous* to that of political revolution.[28] The book takes the form of an encyclopedic accumulation of argumentation in support of that thesis, a point worth noting to the extent that it allows us to situate the micropolitics referred to above, the stubbornly local quality of its effect, in terms of its resistance or unassimilability to just such encyclopedic efforts at totalization.

We return, then, to our question: where does the "writing machine"—the virulent residue of a strongly thematic reading of *Quatrevingt-treize*—escape? For whom—and on what grounds—shall our bell (*tocsin*) fail to toll? Our answer shall be twofold. On the one hand, we shall attempt to inscribe the *tocsin* into Hugo's classic novel of "bells," *Notre-Dame de Paris.* That move is doubly regressive, from 1793 to 1482 in Hugo's fictive history of the West, from 1872 to 1831 in the author's career as a writer. Or perhaps triply so: for to consider *Notre-Dame de Paris* is less to examine a masterpiece of the canon than to re-encounter a childhood classic of the international *bourgeoisie.* The move backward then is inevitably one into the corrupt intimacy of a certain family structure. To observe the *tocsin* exercising its disruptive effects within that monument of edification, *Notre-Dame de Paris,* will thus be to witness a certain corrosive turbulence within the

28. "Une pratique que l'on pourrait comparer à celle de la révolution politique: l'une opère pour le sujet ce que l'autre introduit dans la société." *La Révolution du langage poétique* (Paris: Seuil, 1974), p. 14.

institution of the Family. Indeed, it will be one of the aims of our speculative reading of the novel to demonstrate that just such a convulsion may be the subject *par excellence* of Hugo's book.

But our *tocsin* shall escape "forward" as well. Our reading of *Notre-Dame de Paris* shall simultaneously constitute a reading of one of the most difficult of French theoretical texts, Jacques Derrida's *Glas*. The details of that reading shall emerge gradually, but at this juncture we would suggest that what follows in these pages *reads Glas,* much as *Glas* itself implicitly reads *Thus Spake Zarathustra*: "Vous disposez ici, comme en contrebande, de tout le nécessaire pour une lecture à peu près complète, littéralement littérale, de Zarathoustra. Vous pouvez vérifier."[29] The case of a child's classic repeating the moves of the most advanced analytic discourse is odd indeed. The only parallel imaginable would be Freud's "theory of castration," which, before being Freud's, was the property of its inventor, "Little Hans." For it is an "infantile theory of sexuality" *par excellence*. If we invoke the case of Hans, moreover, it is because the question of "castration"—and its disarticulation—will be at the core of our reading of *Notre Dame de Paris* even as it figures centrally—as the very dimension of centrality—in *Glas*. Indeed, if our reading of Hugo's novel results in constituting it as a premonitory hallucination of Derrida's text, it is perhaps to the extent that we have been able to imagine the child's classic being read by one of the most influential children in the history of the West, Little Hans.

29. *Glas* (Paris: Galilée, 1974), p. 118.

Our *tocsin,* then, will serve pedagogically as an introduction to Derrida's *Glas.* Consider the strangeness of that proposition. A warning bell (*tocsin*) shall serve to prepare not for a danger but for the bell (*glas*) coming after the danger has wreaked its catastrophic effects. In the process the catastrophe itself as event has been lost in a vibratory play between what precedes and follows it. But what if the catastrophe were nothing other than the loss of the event in the centrality of its "eventhood"? What if the "introduction" began to repeat or mime the "event itself" so effectively that the two became indistinguishable in the midst of their immense difference? These questions—about our own undertaking—are as well those which we shall rediscover at the heart of our reading of Hugo.

> As flowers turn toward the sun, by dint of a secret heliotropism the past strives toward that sun which is rising in the sky of history. A historical materialist must be aware of this most inconspicuous of all transformations.   —WALTER BENJAMIN, *Theses on the Philosophy of History*

The title of Hugo's novel is doubly inscribed, for *Notre-Dame de Paris* names both a cathedral and a printed text. Now that situation is worthy of comment to the extent that an important chapter in the novel posits the polemical relation between the two. "Ceci tuera cela," says the fanatical priest Claude Frollo, as he glances from a printed volume to the cathedral; and he elaborates in a premonitory lament on what Benjamin would call "The Work of Art in the Age of Mechanical Reproduction": "le livre tuera l'édifice"

(p. 135).[30] Hugo himself takes up Frollo's theme in the following chapter and meditates at length on the precariousness and inevitable dissolution of architecture, the most primal of arts, in an age of print: "le livre imprimé, ce ver rongeur de l'édifice, la suce et la dévore" (p. 142). Thus the novel which has been acclaimed as an evocation of the cathedral, a celebration of the primal virtues of medieval architecture, is logically concerned with dismantling both cathedral and the art of which it is so glorious a manifestation. *Notre-Dame de Paris* is the name of a war, a polemical field. The title buckles atop a monument—of prose? of stone?—intent on its own destruction. The self-consuming title of *Notre-Dame de Paris* repeats the condition of *Saint-Barthélémy:* at once description and victim of a "massacre." In what follows we shall, then, examine how the writing machine (the printing press) of *Notre-Dame de Paris* repeats, writes, or is written by the "writing machine" (or *tocsin*) of *Quatrevingt-treize* as each escapes from the monument (cathedral or book) that would contain it. *Notre-Dame de Paris:* "Sous la forme imprimerie, la pensée humaine . . . est volatile, insaisissable, indestructible. Elle se mêle à l'air. Du temps de l'architecture, elle se faisait montagne et s'emparait puissamment d'un siècle et d'un lieu. Maintenant elle se fait troupeau d'oiseaux, s'éparpille aux quatre vents, et occupe à la fois tous les points de l'air et de l'espace" (p. 141). *Quatrevingt-treize:* "Page à page, émietté par ces petits doigts acharnés, presque tout l'antique livre

30. Page references in the text are to vol. IV of Hugo, *Oeuvres complètes,* ed. J. Massin (Paris: Club français du livre, 1967).

s'envola dans le vent. Georgette, pensive, regarda ces essaims de petits papiers blancs se disperser à tous les souffles de l'air . . . " (p. 442). Beyond Hugo's efforts to offer a humanistic interpretation of either scene, it is the vulnerability of the masterpiece or cultural monument to a radical form of dispersion that shall concern us and serve as the turbulent medium through which the *tocsin* of Hugo's novel of the Terror may be grafted into the earlier work.

Notre-Dame de Paris may be read as the chronicle of an interruption in the career of the relatively minor character, Pierre Gringoire. He is poet, dramatist, and philosopher, but above all the *author* of his works. The novel begins with Gringoire pressed by the crowd assembled in the Grand' Salle to begin the mystery which he has prepared for Twelfth Night. He cannot resist identifying himself to those near him in the audience: " 'Mes damoiselles, c'est moi qui en suis l'auteur . . . . Je m'appelle Pierre Gringoire.' L'auteur du Cid n'eût pas dit avec plus de fierté: Pierre Corneille" (p. 38). The author is thus a certain identity of self incarnate in a proper name. And the humiliation that follows is visited above all on that name. For soon the performance ("la représentation"), after several minor disruptions, will be permanently and ruinously interrupted: "Avec quelle amertume, il voyait s'écrouler pièce à pièce tout son échafaudage de gloire et de poésie!" (p. 50). Now the reason for the definitive interruption is twofold. On the one hand, a contest of ugliness is initiated to celebrate the *Fête des Fous*. The winner is the deaf bell-ringer Quasimodo, and the surprise that occasions his triumph is worth noting:

"L'acclamation fut unanime. On se précipita vers la chapelle. On en fit sortir en triomphe le bienheureux pape des fous. Mais c'est alors que la surprise et l'admiration furent à leur comble. La grimace était son visage .... Ou plutôt toute sa personne était une grimace" (p. 53). Thus the "representation" has been interrupted by an instance that breaks with the relation of subordination between face and grimace, reality and parody, thing and sign, which is constitutive of the concept of representation. The second and definitive disruption is the announcement that La Esmeralda is in the square. As the crowd rushes out of the auditorium, Gringoire is left to puzzle over his humiliation: "Mais je veux que le diable m'écorche si je comprends ce qu'ils veulent dire avec leur Esmeralda! Qu'est-ce que c'est que ce mot d'abord? c'est de l'égyptiaque!" (p. 56). Soon, however, we discover that La Esmeralda is the name of a gypsy ("égyptienne") dancer performing in the Place de Grève, that sinister square, Hugo reminds us, that would later be the last refuge of public executions by the guillotine.

We may begin, then, to constitute an associative chain: Quasimodo's split tympanum, a core of deafness generative of the peeling bells; a disruption of the relation constitutive of representation; Egyptian; guillotine. Together they serve to cut short Gringoire's performance ("représentation"), to drive a breach into a certain circuit of communion with self: "Toute communication était interceptée entre son noeud et son dénouement" (p. 56). Gringoire's bitter complaint at the fickleness of his audience: "ils viennent pour entendre un mystère, et n'en écoutent rien!" (p. 56).

Through our associative chain and its action, through
the poet's lament, are we not already in that chapter of
Quatrevingt-treize entitled, in what is virtually a Latin
transcription of Gringoire's line: "Aures habet, et non
audiet"? Might the clapper of our *tocsin* be beating
silently forty years prior to Hugo's final novel in
Notre-Dame de Paris?

We shall continue to follow Gringoire in his humiliation before offering our answer. The poet turns
philosopher in his disappointment: "La philosophie du
reste était son seul refuge, car il ne savait où loger" (p.
57). He wanders through the streets of Paris and manages to get lost as he follows the innocent but seductive
Esmeralda through "ce dédale inextricable de ruelles,
de carrefours et de culs de sac . . . mille circuits qui
revenaient sans cesse sur eux-mêmes" (p. 69). The
philosopher in the labyrinth, however, reaches his
point of maximal disorientation when he finds
himself—prisoner—in the thieves' city of La Cour des
Miracles: "fourmilère d'éclopés" (p. 74) . . . "un
nouveau monde, inconnu, inouï, difforme, reptile,
fourmillant, fantastique" (p. 75). We may perhaps
evoke the qualities of the Cour by suggesting that in
describing it Hugo plainly drew on the same imaginative and rhetorical resources as in presenting that other
pocket of fascinating and anarchical abjection, the
Vendée. La Cour des Miracles, Hugo's medieval un-
derworld, is the Vendée of *Notre-Dame de Paris*. The
philosopher's reaction is one of stunned disbelief: "Si
je suis, cela est-il? si cela est, suis-je?" (p. 76). Soon,
however, the "author" is faced with a choice: he will
either join the thieves, become an "argotier," or be

executed. The test of admission consists in pickpocket-
ing a dummy, strewn with bells, hung from a
gallows—without ringing the bells. If he does ring
them, he will replace the dummy in the noose. To
undergo the linguistic transformation from author or
master of the language to anonymous practitioner of
argot is thus tantamount to *stealing the sound of—or
from—a series of bells,* manipulating a vast system of
bells *silently.* It would appear then that Gringoire's life
will depend on his ability to execute the task that Hugo
managed in the apparently peripheral episode of
Quatrevingt-treize with which we began our analysis.

He fails to and is saved only by Hugo's sentimental-
ity, that is, by La Esmeralda's willingness to take
chastely as her husband the somewhat dilapidated
philosopher. Thus is the philosopher (dis)integrated
into the den of thieves. Later in the novel, we find him
performing ludicrously as a street clown, explaining to
Claude Frollo: "Me voilà en habit d'histrion comme
saint Genest. Que voulez-vous? c'est une éclipse" (p.
185). But his role in the remainder of the novel is
minor, reduced to serving as the dupe of Frollo in his
nefarious plot. At the novel's end he returns to his
career as an author, composing tragedies: "C'est ce
qu'il appelait *avoir fait une fin tragique*" (p. 341).

The action of the novel may thus be considered as an
interruption in the career of an author, in the life of
literature. And that pause, which began as a disruption
of (a) "representation," found its ideal form in the
act of "stealing the sound" of a series of bells. The time
of the novel would seem to be generated by the silent
oscillation of the *tocsin* of 1793. But what of the action

proper? For Gringoire it is structured by a single word:
"La Esmeralda! . . . . ce mot magique nouait tous les
souvenirs de sa journée" (p. 83). La Esmeralda is then
less a character than a nodal term recurring in his life
with labyrinthine insistence. But to the extent that a
certain love or desire for La Esmeralda motivates the
other (principal) characters in the book, we would
suggest that she "knots" the action for all concerned.
Thus the case of Claude Frollo, the somber archdeacon
of Notre-Dame, consumed by two passions: alchemy
and his lust for La Esmeralda. Note that in his fanatical
rigor he may be superimposed as textual function on
Cimourdain, and his twin passions on those of the
délégué civil for the Revolution and Gauvain. As for
Quasimodo, Frollo's adopted servant, "borgne,
boîteux, bossu," he is distracted from his beloved bells
only by the sight of La Esmeralda, and his principal
actions in the novel are dictated by his love for her.
Thus is La Esmeralda loved—differently—by three
men (Gringoire, Frollo, Quasimodo), and thus is the
action of the novel dictated in its ramifications by the
fascination exercised by "l'Egyptienne."

But La Esmeralda in the text is first of all a word
("égyptiaque") to be deciphered, an impropriety in
the system of nomenclature demanding an act of
exegesis. Gringoire eventually asks his bride why she
bears her strange name: "Elle tira de son sein une espèce de petit sachet oblong suspendu à son cou par une
chaîne d'adrézach. Ce sachet exhalait une forte odeur
de camphre. Il était recouvert de soie verte, et portait à
son centre une grosse verroterie verte, imitant
l'émeraude . . . .—C'est peut-être à cause de cela, dit-

elle" (p. 88). The emerald is fake: *toc*. It is suspended at the level of her breasts: *seins*. As she dances it no doubt oscillates between them: *toque-sein*. La Esmeralda, a false name, a forged signature: *toc-seing*.

The question of the meaning of a name arises again in the case of Phoebus, the dashing young soldier who callously seduces and abandons the enamoured gypsy. Phoebus, La Esmeralda is told, means *sun*. She is, then, in love with the sun, with a character so lacking in depth, so psychologically thin that we are inclined to describe him as a superstar. Indeed La Esmeralda is nothing so much as the frustrated desire for the evanescent Phoebus. Her characteristic gesture in the novel is to turn desperately, at times disastrously, toward Phoebus and to fail to encounter him: "La danseuse ne tambourinait pas en ce moment. Elle tourna la tête vers le point d'où lui venait cet appel, son regard se fixa sur Phoebus, et elle s'arrêta tout court" (p. 179). And again at the end of the novel: "Elle se leva, et avant que sa mère eût pu l'en empêcher, elle s'était jetée à la lucarne en criant:—Phoebus! à moi, mon Phoebus! . . . Phoebus n'y était plus. Il venait de tourner au galop l'angle de la rue de la Coutellerie" (p. 331). La Esmeralda is a heliotrope.

Consider our point of departure: a disruption in representation brought about by a series of elements which seemed so many components of the elaborate writing machine—or *tocsin*—of *Quatrevingt-treize*. Whereupon we discovered that for the philosopher to pass *fully* into the realm of *argot* was to steal the sound of—or from—a bell. Now that we have examined the action that transpires within this hiatus in Gringoire's career as author, we see that it is motivated by what we have constructed as a *toque-sein/toc-sein/toc-seing*. In brief, our analysis, at this stage, has taken the precise form of *stealing the sound of a bell (tocsin)*. Such are the ruses of interpretation imposed by the text, such the perversity of language in the realm of *argot*.

Our *tocsin* is as well a heliotrope, a movement toward the sun (Phoebus) that fails to attain it, a flawed turning toward the source: a blot against the sun. But that was precisely the situation of the *tocsin* in "Aures habet, et non audiet." It figured there as an intermittent blackness silently blocking out the sun. Pierre Gringoire as clown: "Que voulez-vous? c'est une éclipse" (p. 185). Heliotrope/tocsin; flower/bell: we encounter here a movement of reversal of shape which is that of the oscillating bell itself. A second meaning of heliotrope is bloodstone. The *Oxford English Dictionary* quotes Philemon Holland: "The pretious stone Heliotropium is a deepe greene in manner of a leeke garnished with veins of bloud." La Esmeralda is, then, a heliotrope swollen animate. Having progressed from La Esmeralda to *tocsin* to heliotrope, we find we have come full circle with the return of a "deepe greene" stone. Our writing machine is then the pure and unending movement of metaphoricity from term to term in our circular chain. But these results converge with those of Derrida's remarkable inquiry into the status of metaphor in the history of philosophy. From Aristotle to Nietzsche, he demonstrates that the metaphor of the heliotrope, a failed movement toward an elusive source, is the metaphor of metaphoricity itself: "Métaphore veut donc dire héliotrope, à la fois mouvement tourné vers le soleil et mouvement tournant du soleil."[31] Heliotropism is for Derrida the infinitely cascading medium of metaphoricity within which a certain non-teleological death of philosophy may be effected. For us it takes its place through La Esmeralda in a complex writing machine. But to invoke such a machine in the context of *Notre-Dame de Paris* is inevitably to conjure up the printing presses of "Ceci tuera cela," that is, to work toward the undermining of that other onto-theological monument, the cathedral itself.

La Esmeralda as character leads both Claude Frollo and Quasimodo to their doom. But as writing machine she visits a more threatening death on these characters. For brought to a certain pitch the primordial metaphoricity we have invoked is corrosive of that minimum of homogeneity without which the very notion of "character" loses its consistency. The case of the archdeacon is particularly instructive. At an important juncture in the novel, Claude, brooding with a colleague in alchemy in his study within the cathedral, observes a fly foiled in an attempted flight out of the edifice toward the sun. It is caught in a spider's web and quickly devoured. Claude's impassioned commentary:

. . . voilà un symbole de tout. Elle [la mouche] vole, elle est joyeuse, elle vient de naître; oh! oui, mais qu'elle se heurte à la rosace fatale, l'araignée en sort, l'araignée hideuse! Pauvre danseuse! pauvre mouche prédestinée! Maître Jacques, laissez faire! c'est la fatalité! Hélas! Claude, tu es l'araignée.

31. "La Mythologie blanche" in *Marges* (Paris: Minuit, 1972), p. 299.

Claude, tu es la mouche aussi! Tu volais à la science, à la lumière, au soleil, tu n'avais souci que d'arriver au grand air, au grand jour de la vérité éternelle; mais, en te précipitant vers la lucarne éblouissante qui donne sur l'autre monde, sur le monde de la clarté, de l'intelligence et de la science, mouche aveugle, docteur insensé, tu n'as pas vu cette subtile toile d'araignée tendue par le destin entre la lumière et toi, tu t'y es jeté à corps perdu, misérable fou, et maintenant tu te débats, la tête brisée et les ailes arrachées, entre les antennes de fer de la fatalité!—Maître Jacques! maître Jacques! laissez faire l'araignée. (p. 201)

Claude Frollo is, then, caught up in the heliotropic metaphor. And the failure inscribed in that movement is here attributed to the web—or text—of fate. But *fate* itself, in its written form, is, of course, a highly charged word in the novel. The preface evokes the disappearance of the word ANANKE etched into the wall of the cathedral, and concludes: "C'est sur ce mot qu'on a fait ce livre" (p. 20). Writing the novel is thus tantamount to restoring that word or text (the web of *fate*), the medium through which the heliotrope consummates its failure.

We should note here how closely Frollo's heliotropic scenario prefigures a crucial subsequent episode in the novel: La Esmeralda's seduction by Phoebus and victimization by Claude. And yet the point to be made in the case cited is that Claude is *both* fly and spider. At this point in the novel he is less a figure in an allegorical drama than the sheer capacity for displacement in a fantasmatic scenario. And it is that radical metaphoricity which is a measure of the havoc wreaked by the heliotrope on what one no longer feels quite justified in calling the "character" of Claude Frollo.

And what of Quasimodo? The reader's experience of the novel is marked by a growing realization of a certain substitutability of the hunchback for La Esmeralda. For Quasimodo was the child abandoned by the gypsies in place of the abducted La Esmeralda. Even at the level of their names one begins to see a certain contamination of the sublime by the grotesque, a surprising equivalence between the two. For Quasimodo, we are reminded, means "à peu près" (p. 117). La Esmeralda is addressed by her beloved, who can never quite recall her name, as Similar (p. 239). Similar, Quasimodo: close, but not quite. The novel thus elaborates a surprising interchangeability between the epitomes of the sublime and the grotesque. This is underscored in the chapter entitled "Une Larme pour une goutte d'eau" (p. 167). When La Esmeralda brings water to the pilloried Quasimodo, he emits a telling tear: "Alors, dans cet oeil jusque-là si sec et si brûlé, on vit rouler une grosse larme qui tomba lentement le long de ce visage difforme et longtemps contracté par le désespoir" (p. 172). The episode is a sentimental illustration of the process Freud termed "anaclisis [*Anlehnung*]": the movement whereby a fantasmatic and "partial" object is generated "marginally" in excess of the satisfaction of an instinct.[32] The very subjectivity of Quasimodo is metonymically focused on that drop and its substitutions. For when *his* turn comes to reciprocate the gypsy's kindness, Hugo evokes his exploit as follows:

32. For a discussion of *Anlehnung,* see Chapter I of Jean Laplanche, *Vie et mort en psychanalyse* (Paris: Flammarion, 1970). Translated into English with an introduction by J. Mehlman (Baltimore: Johns Hopkins, 1976).

Il enjamba la balustrade de la galerie, saisit la corde des pieds, des genoux et des mains, puis on le vit couler sur la façade, comme une goutte de pluie qui glisse le long d'une vitre, courir vers les deux bourreaux avec la vitesse d'un chat tombé d'un toit, les terrasser sous deux poings énormes, enlever l'égyptienne d'une main, comme un enfant sa poupée, et d'un seul élan rebondir jusque dans l'église, en élevant la jeune fille au-dessus de sa tête, et en criant d'une voix formidable: Asile! (p. 247)

At his most intense, Quasimodo is nothing but the sheer mobility of that "partial object" in its circuit of exchange: raindrop for tear (for a drop of water). Thus it is that La Esmeralda-Similar, our "writing machine," continues to tear apart the characters of the novel. We have already seen Claude Frollo inscribed as heliotrope. It remains for us to see Quasimodo transformed into a silent *tocsin*.

That operation occurs in one of the most memorable chapters of the book, one in which Hugo presents what I should be inclined to call an exemplary *theory* of textuality. "*Théorie*: (repris au xviiie siècle au grec *theoria,* 'procession'). *Antiq.* Députation envoyée par une ville à une fête solenelle.—*Par ext.* Groupe de personnes qui s'avancent les unes derrière les autres."[33] We shall do well to adopt this entirely secondary meaning of theory for it admirably captures the silent procession of *truands,* the delegates of the city of thieves, as they cross the bridges of the Seine to converge upon the cathedral: "L'immense multitude parut se former en colonne . . . . Dix minutes après, les cavaliers du guet s'enfuyaient épouvantés devant une longue pro-

33. Robert, *Dictionnaire de la langue française.*

cession d'hommes noirs et silencieux qui descendait
vers le Pont-au-Change . . ." (p. 283). Such is this
army of the night, "cohue de morts, muette, impalpa-
ble . . . effrayant troupeau d'hommes et de femmes en
haillons, armés de faulx, de piques, de serpes . . ." (p.
284). Its members have come to besiege the masterpiece, cathect the cathedral: to liberate La Esmeralda, a
certain movement of metaphoricity imprisoned
within the monument. Now what is remarkable is the
form that the onslaught eventually takes. The *truands*
scale the walls of the cathedral: "Aucun moyen de ré-
sister à cette marée ascendante de faces épouvantables.
La fureur faisait rutiler ces figures farouches . . . . On
eut dit que quelque autre église avait envoyé à l'assaut
de Notre-Dame ses gorgones, ses dogues, ses drées, ses
démons, ses sculptures les plus fantastiques. C'était
comme une couche de monstres vivants sur les
monstres de pierre de la façade" (p. 294). What we are
invited to witness is not a penetration to the heart of
the masterpiece but a bizarre simulation of its surface.
But what is our *tocsin* if not a certain silent vibration cut
off from its *end* as sound? And what our heliotrope if
not a wavering that fails to attain its source? Indeed the
"practice" which is indistinguishable from our own
textual "theory" has consisted in playing off surface
(of *Quatrevingt-treize*) against surface (of *Notre-Dame de
Paris*), of replicating the *tocsin* of the later novel,
through the most rigorously superficial of re-
semblances, into a perfectly monstrous *toque-sein*. It is
in that context that we are inclined to consider the
crowning image of the entire sequence. Quasimodo, in
the delusion that he is protecting La Esmeralda from

her would-be ravishers, prepares a fire atop the cathedral to melt the lead he eventually pours on the besiegers of the cathedral. "Et parmi ces monstres ainsi réveillés de leur sommeil de pierre par cette flamme, par ce bruit, il y en avait un qui marchait et qu'on voyait de temps en temps passer sur le front ardent du bûcher comme une chauve-souris devant une chandelle" (p. 290. The odd alternation of light and eclipse is metaphorized as a "phare étrange" and greeted by the assembled outlaws with a "crainte religieuse" (p. 290). But the object of this terror reproduces quite precisely the configuration of the silent *tocsin* of *Quatrevingt-treize*. The image in the earlier novel comes as the culmination of a series of protective strikes by Quasimodo from above: ". . . la grêle de moellons commença à tomber, et il leur sembla [aux truands] que l'église se démolissait d'elle-même sur leur tête" (p. 289). Quasimodo become *tocsin* is thus the goal of a silent procession, of a "theory" of textuality. Become "writing machine," he presides blindly, above all deafly, over the very process whereby the cathedral seems to dismantle itself.

Such as well is the goal of our own textual theory: a perverse replication or repetition-in-difference of the surface, making the limits of the masterpiece tremble in a movement of silent alternation. It is an effort to coincide with that infinitely superficial stratum of the text whereby it begins undoing or dismantling itself. It calculates its effects solely in exhilaration, in the energy released by the transformations achieved. But this theory is a practice as well, or rather, it is insufficiently stable to be able to sustain that metalinguistic distance

without which the distinction theory/practice is unthinkable. As Hugo has it in *Notre-Dame de Paris,* the
outlaws, in their very effort to liberate that dimension
of radical metaphoricity (La Esmeralda) from the masterpiece, simultaneously fail to attain their object and
find *themselves* appearing as grotesque duplications (or
metaphors) of the surface of the cathedral (as masterpiece). Our (Hugo's?) "theory," then, is a practice that
may be defined through the perverse rigor with which
it *misses* its object. To borrow a pun from *Les Misérables,* it is less a philosophy of literature than a *filousophie*
of textuality.

Now oddly enough the entire sequence initiated by
the "theory" of outlaws is described by Hugo as premonitory of 1789. For the storming of the cathedral is
observed with remarkable calm by Louis XI from his
apartment in the Bastille. His composure is the result
of a misinterpretation. He believes that the populace is
attacking not the royal cathedral but a feudal bailiwick:
"Ah! mon peuple! voilà donc que tu m'aides enfin à
l'écroulement des seigneuries!" (p. 309). While still
under this misconception, the king has the following
exchange with a Flemish visitor attuned to the mood
of the people:

> Je dis, sire, que vous avez peut-être raison, que l'heure du
> peuple n'est pas venue chez vous.
>   Louis XI le regarda avec son oeil pénétrant.
>   —Et quand viendra cette heure, maître?
>   —Vous l'entendrez sonner.
>   —A quelle horloge, s'il vous plaît?
>   Coppenole avec sa contenance tranquille et rustique fit
> approcher le roi de la fenêtre. —Ecoutez, sire! Il y a ici un

donjon, un beffroi, des canons, des bourgeois, des soldats. Quand le beffroi bourdonnera, quand les canons gronderont, quand le donjon croulera à grand bruit, quand bourgeois et soldats hurleront et s'entretueront, c'est l'heure qui sonnera. (p. 310)

Shortly thereafter Louis is shocked to discover that the object of the attack is his cathedral and moves to crush the revolt pitilessly.

The besieging of the masterpiece by the most heterogeneous elements in society is thus plainly, for Hugo, a premonition of the Revolution. One senses in this somewhat improbable parallel between the events of 1482 and 1789 that liberal teleology of history which would see in the year of the bourgeois revolution a culmination of all that preceded it. But such a juxtaposition of the two years has a precise basis in the textual activity of our author. For shortly after the completion of *Notre-Dame de Paris,* he was, in *Littérature et philosophie mêlées* (1834), to reproduce the constellation of traits that had crystallized as Quasimodo in the figure of the great orator of the revolution, Mirabeau: "homme avorté," "créature disloquée," "mâle monstrueux."[34] Like Quasimodo, Mirabeau is associated with the spirit of the People. The lawyer of Aix was, in fact, for Hugo "the most complete symbol" of the People in 1789. The difference, of course, is in the degree of articulateness of the two. The mythographers of Hugo's *oeuvre* join the poet here in his teleology of 1789. Thus P. Albouy: "Au xve siécle, le peuple, difforme encore et proche de la brute, ne sait pas parler. Mais son jour viendra, prédit par le chaus-

34. *Littérature et philosophie mêlées* in *Oeuvres complètes,* vol. V, p. 197.

setier gantois, Jacques Coppenole, qui prophétise, devant Louis XI, la chute de la Bastille."[35] The *end* of
history is incarnate in the *logos,* the "Verbe" emergent
at last from the deformed mouth of Mirabeau. The
virtual muteness of Quasimodo is a falling short of that
phonic plenitude.

But what of 1793? Our reading of *Quatrevingt-treize*
mediated nothing so much as a deconstruction of the
logocentic scheme which Albouy has (justifiably)
extracted from his juxtaposition of Quasimodo and
Mirabeau. The later novel would afford us the means
to reinscribe the relation between the silence of the
bell-ringer and the eloquence of the orator. The cult of
1789 in Hugo would serve to repress the textuality of
1793. We have seen Quasimodo become silent *tocsin*
atop Notre-Dame. Hugo interprets that warning sig-
nal affirmatively as an anticipation of the storming of
the Bastille: only then will the hour of the people have
sounded. But in our retrospective reading the *tocsin* of
the earlier novel is clearly a component in the "writing
machine" of 1793. Indeed, in an important way, the
"warning bell" of 1482 *repeats* that of the later novel. In
a certain undecidability between the mute bell of 1482
(anticipating 1789) and that of 1793 (the death knell of
the liberal revolution), the ideals of 1789, logocentic
and *bourgeois* through and through, are disoriented,
made to suffer a devastating disarticulation. An entire
teleology of history is disrupted. Such is the unin-
tended force of Hugo's textuality. It is to a final effort
to domesticate that energy within *Notre-Dame de Paris*
that we now shall turn.

35. *La Création mythologique chez Victor Hugo* (Paris: Corti, 1963),
p. 216.

In the benighted battle between Quasimodo and the *truands,* the struggle for possession of La Esmeralda, . . . she escapes. Or rather, she is abducted by a desperate Claude Frollo in disguise. As the novel draws to a close, the *end* of her evasion becomes clear: she is moving toward a discovery of her own identity. The cascading movement of metaphoricity itself (*tocsin* and heliotrope), crystallized in the imaginary unity of a character, would here be reduced, come to rest in a revelation of selfhood. A discussion of the circumstances of that discovery requires reference to a character we have not yet mentioned. For after Claude Frollo despairs of ever winning the affection of La Esmeralda, he delivers her into the punitive custody of Gudule, while he makes off to fetch the royal authorities. Gudule is a wretched penitent who has retreated in misery from the world after her one joy in life, an infant daughter, was kidnapped by a band of gypsies. Her one vestige of the child is a single slipper which she now cherishes in the penitent's cave she occupies in Paris. Above that retreat are inscribed the edifying words: TU, ORA. But in view of the sinister character of the cave, the public has transformed those words into a demeaning name for the retreat: "Trou aux rats" (p. 154). The one emotion Gudule still seems capable of is rage at the most visible gypsy in the book, La Esmeralda, whom she frequently sees dancing in the square adjacent to her cell. Whence Claude's confidence in delivering La Esmeralda into Gudule's custody. Events move rapidly toward the melodramatic moment of recognition. Gudule shrieks her rage, then her desperate love for her child, and finally manifests the slipper. Whereupon:

—Montrez-moi ce soulier, dit l'égyptienne en tressaillant.
Dieu! Dieu! Et en même temps, de la main qu'elle avait libre,
elle ouvrait vivement le petit sachet orné de verroterie verte
qu'elle portait au cou.

—Va! va! grommelait Gudule, fouille ton amulette du
démon! Tout à coup elle s'interrompit, trembla de tout son
corps et cria avec une voix qui venait du plus profond des
entrailles:—Ma fille!

L'égyptienne venait de tirer du sachet un petit soulier
absolument pareil à l'autre. (p. 326)

Victor Hugo hélàs. . . Before pursuing the analysis it is
worth while pausing to savor the intolerable sentimen-
tality of the scene. Shortly thereafter, the royal guard
arrives led by none other than Phoebus. La Esmeralda,
secreted in the recesses of Gudule's cave, cannot resist a
last heliotropic move. In a passage already quoted, she
betrays herself by turning toward Phoebus and shout-
ing his name—just as he disappears from view. In this
final heliotropism, what is lost is both object
(Phoebus) and subject: as a result of her act, she is
captured and soon put to death.

How are we to read this final sequence? We may
begin by noting how closely the pair of slippers cor-
responds to that dimension which Lévi-Strauss, then
Lacan have isolated as the *symbolique*. E. Ortigues'
evocation of the tessera of antiquity is a convenient
guide here: "Le symbole est un gage de reconnaissance,
un objet coupé en deux et distribué entre deux par-
tenaires alliés qui devaient conserver chacun leur part
et la transmettre à leurs descendants, de telle sorte que
ces éléments complémentaires à nouveau rapprochés,
permettaient par leur ajustement réciproque de faire
reconnaître les porteurs et d'attester les liens d'alliance

contractés antérieurement. Le *sum-bolon* consiste dans
la corrélation entre des éléments sans valeur isolée,
mais dont la réunion (*sum-ballô*) ou l'ajustement réciproque permet à deux alliés de se faire reconnaître
comme tels . . . ."[36] A first reading of the novel's conclusion, then: to be confronted with the contents of the
toque-sein, to discover the *identity* of a character who
has gone by the palpably false name—*toc-seing*—of La
Esmeralda is to encounter a certain ludicrousness of
the scenario informing the very notion of the *symbolique.* It is perhaps as well to prefer the receptacle, the
residue: to affirm the *tocsin* or writing machine as containing or exceeding the *symbolique.* It is perhaps even
to suspect that Hugo invites as much in his plotting of
La Esmeralda's last "heliotropism," a thoroughly
metaphorical movement fundamentally destructive of
her newly acquired identity.

The *symbolique* of the structuralists is that dimension
of unconscious structure through which the values and
desires of a society are transmitted. As such, it occupies
within the thought of our contemporaries a role not
unlike that other structure bearing and preserving the
traditions of a culture: the cathedral of Notre-Dame in
Hugo's novel. In positing the *symbolique* as contained
by the writing machine, may we not then be dealing
with a phenomenon analogous to that odd replication
of the surface of the cathedral through which that
monument was besieged? Such is the hypothesis I shall
attempt to sustain in the ensuing analysis. In fact, I shall
be discussing the "besieging" of a specific component
of the *symbolique,* the concept of "castration." For that

36. *Le Discours et le symbole* (Paris: Aubier, 1962), p. 60.

category, originally the theme of an "infantile sexual theory," is the cornerstone of the *symbolique*. The castration complex, coming at the culmination of the Oedipal crisis, marks the child's entry into the intersubjective structure of exchange known as the *symbolique*. To exceed and dislocate the notion of castration, to work one's way out of the order it *structures,* is thus perhaps to move in an analytic medium that can no longer be called "structuralist."

As our analysis of the textual "theory" of *Notre-Dame de Paris* converges with the issues of a crucially contemporary debate, we should do well to situate briefly the terms of that crux. In the interpretation of Freud that has loomed so large in the intellectual life of France in the last ten years, the notion of "castration" has enjoyed special privilege. The specific reasons for its attractiveness are clear. It is a theory of (sexual) difference, catastrophic to every image of (ego's) integrity, a cornerstone of the structural unconscious. There were few categories in the history of Western thought better suited to the structuralist project than Freud's "castration." Indeed, when asked informally by bewildered Americans what French structuralism was, after all, all about, one was hard put to find a more usefully concise response than the flippant observation that there were two kinds of people in the world: those who when they read Freud find the most potentially liberating or exhilarating category to be bisexuality and those for whom it was castration. The Americans were among the former; the French (structuralists) among the latter. Lacan and those around him were distinguished by their willingness to take seriously Freud's remark that the castration complex was the "bedrock" beyond which one could not go.

Yet whatever the analytic yields accruing to the French from their privileging of "castration," the affirmation of that category entails a major drawback for any intellectual enterprise aspiring to a stance that might be called radical. For to the extent that the castration complex marks the (logical) moment of the subject's insertion into structure, any affirmation of castration runs the severe risk of sounding flatly adaptative. (Indeed, the heavily normative aspects of Freud's theory of sexuality are intimately bound up with the castration complex.) Much of the aftermath of structuralism may be read in terms of degrees of ambivalence toward the duplicity of castration: at once radical theory of *difference* and medium through which subject is made to adapt to structure. Thus Deleuze and Guattari, for example, in a celebrated volume, have attempted to laugh away castration—and, ultimately, Freud with it—as the "ideology of lack."[37] The risk run in such a move is that in writing off Freud, one may quite simply have eliminated the interpretative medium in which the question of sexuality may be *thought* with maximal intensity. One suspects that if "castration," with all the traps that it poses, is to be "overcome," it will be by engaging the intricacies of Freud's texts and not by laughing them away. For that reason, our own approach to the fundamentally open question of castration shall be through a consideration of the key discoveries of an inquiry far less publicized than that of Deleuze and Guattari, the lectures on cast-

37. *L'Anti-Oedipe* (Paris: Minuit, 1972), p. 71.

ration delivered by Jean Laplanche.[38] For Laplanche, I
believe, by dealing with the letter of Freud's text, has
waged the most convincing combat against the interpretative tendency that would see in "castration" the
repressed *par excellence*. Whereas the authors of the
Anti-Oedipe would laugh castration away, Laplanche
manages to retain it . . . in the very element of its
ludicrousness.

It will perhaps be objected that we are moving all
too rapidly away from our reading of Hugo. But, in
fact, our reason for invoking the most striking results
of Laplanche's analyses is that they provide a remarkably efficient summary of our own conclusions regarding Hugo. We approach here a certain withering of
the all too academic question of the relation between
Psychoanalysis and Literature. For our answer to that
question of theory will be a demonstration of the way
in which a transformation of psychoanalysis may be
made to help effect a certain displacement of literature
as well. The abstract problem of theory gives way to a
concrete textual analysis that is undecidably psychoanalytic or literary. "Psychoanalysis" and "Literature": terms to be inscribed on the "opposite" sides
of a Möbius strip.

What follows, then, are three important devel-
opments from Laplanche's ongoing inquiry into the
perverse rigor with which Freud's most virulent discoveries are perpetually escaping him, undergoing re-

38. Laplanche's lectures have appeared over the last few years,
under the titles "Les Normes morales et sociales, leur impact dans
la topique subjective" and "La Castration, ses précurseurs, son
destin," in *Bulletin de Psychologie,* Nos. 306–308, 311–312 (1972–
74).

pression. They turn on the question of castration and may be seen to be literally inscribed in Hugo's text.

I.

A prerequisite for an understanding of castration is an examination of the crucial shift in Freud's theory of anxiety. The initial "naive" theory, elaborated at the beginning of the century in the context of a discussion of "actual neuroses," posits anxiety as a deviant form of discharge of dammed up libido. The theory is economic and comes close to being purely physiological in orientation. In the absence of libidinal discharge, the ego is threatened with submergence by a free-floating form of affect, a tension virtually without quality: anxiety. It is what Freud calls a poison, a toxin.

For that reason, it should be noted, "actual neuroses" were not deemed particularly amenable to psychoanalytic treatment. Unlike the "psycho-neuroses," to which they were opposed, they could not be traced etiologically to some motivating occurrence in the patient's past. Oddly enough, the theory of anxiety does not become fully "psycho-analytic" until the emergence of the second, more "sophisticated" theory in 1924. Anxiety was then integrated into a theory of defense, more historical than economic in character. It existed above all as "signal-anxiety," a distressing warning of some objective danger which, like a vaccination, would mobilize the defenses of the "psychical organism." Anxiety was no longer the result of repression but the motivating force behind it. To the extent that the prototype of such a danger might be the submergence of the infant at birth through a rush of energy, a virtual self-intoxication, the first theory might still function significantly within, or behind, the second. But gradually the peril *par excellence* was posited by Freud to be castration: "a true external danger."[39] The first theory was deemed "superficial," and partially abandoned. Anxiety was not essentially a poison, a toxin; it was a warning-signal, a tocsin.

We return now to the early theory, specifically to its structure: the liberation of a form of free-floating affect through deviation from a process of instinctual gratification. For in its structure, the "naive" theory reproduces that of one of the most potent and little noticed conceptual configurations in Freud's theory of sexuality: that of *Anlehnung* (anaclisis), the movement, in the *Three Essays,* whereby unconscious sexuality itself (as *Trieb* or drive) is generated as a free-floating form of affect through deviation from a process of instinctual gratification.[40] At the level of structure, then, the first theory begins to appear far less naive.

A second remark on the early theory: within the context of the "toxic" interpretation of anxiety, Freud posited a specific mechanism of defense, phobia. It consists in the focusing of anxiety on some purely arbitrary, external reality perceived as a danger. The prototype would be Little Hans' fear of being bitten by horses. A phobia, in fact, is capable of structuring the entirety of the subject's perception of time and space around the elected object.

It is at this point that the most surprising reversal

39. *Inhibitions, Symptoms, and Anxiety* in the *Standard Edition of the Complete Psychological Works of Sigmund Freud,* vol. XX, ed. J. Strachey (London: Hogarth, 1959), p. 126.
40. See footnote 32 above.

may be operated. For consider: (1) the latent "sophisti-
cation" of the "naive" theory as a structural repetition
of *Anlehnung*; (2) the perfectly futile, unreal, and increasingly rare nature of the castratory scenario that
Freud posits as the grounding reality for his later
theory of anxiety; (3) the dimension of phobia within
the earlier formulation as a theory of imaginary dan-
gers forged in order to focus, bind, and externalize the
free-floating affect of anxiety. Taken together these
three elements lead us to the speculative conclusion
that the entire second theory, centered as it is on the
"true external danger" of castration, is interpretable as
a phobic formation within Freud's own discourse. The
rational fear of father's knife, posited by Freud, is every
bit as ludicrous as Hans' fear of horses. Whereupon we
would suggest that the second theory of anxiety functions as a restricted economy within the general
economy of the first, that the first, once interpreted,
mediates nothing so much as a theory of the inevitabil-
ity of the error entailed by the second. The second
theory, in brief, is the form taken by the repression of
the first, a repression which the historians of psychoanalysis have helped only to consolidate.

But what is Victor Hugo's relation to all this? Our
point of departure was the joining of La Esmeralda's
slippers, the scenario informing the *symbolique*. Castration, we have said, is the cornerstone of the structural unconscious. Our reaction to the episode in Hugo
was embarrassment. The result of the analysis of Freud
just undertaken was the affirmation of a certain (phobic) ludicrousness of the castratory scenario as the second theory of anxiety came to be centered on it. La
Esmeralda drew her slipper out of what a certain silent

contamination allowed us to call *tocsin, toque-sein, toc-seing:* a writing machine. It was that metaphorical duplicity of the container that led us to posit the writing machine as *exceeding* the dimension of the *symbolique*. In our reading of Freud, what allowed us to dismantle castration, to intuit a certain ridiculousness in the way it functions, was the odd shift in Freud's theory of anxiety, the bizarre interplay between anxiety as toxin and anxiety as tocsin. But what is the toxic element in Freud which we came to affirm as constitutive of a general economy if not the free-floating play of unbound affect as it shifts from representation to representation? To say as much, to invoke a silent gliding of terms in relation to their (affective) meanings— say, tocsin replacing toxin as the "meaning" of anxiety—is to sense the extent to which Freud's own text at its most intense functions as a (theory of a) marvelously duplicitous writing machine. We have besieged "castration" much as Hugo's *truands* besieged the cathedral or as the *tocsin* contained the *symbolique*: by giving full play to a certain shiftiness in the apparently secondary element of castration *anxiety,* by doubling the surface. If castration, nevertheless, emerges from this analysis as a necessary construct (or phobia), it will be in the restricted sense in which *Notre-Dame de Paris,* a printed text, may be regarded, despite "Ceci tuera cela," as intended to glorify another construct: Notre-Dame de Paris.

II.

With the passing of the castration complex, in Freud's scheme, the "superego" comes into existence. Now, along with that interpretative tendency in

psychoanalysis that would delibidinize anxiety, turn it
into a displaced fear, there is a pressure to see in the
superego an almost abstract system of logical and ethical imperatives. For if anxiety can be reduced to a fear
of punishment by castration, what would be inter-
nalized as superego would be a law—or laws—
sustained by that fear. It is in this context that we
would consider briefly Laplanche's discussion of the
Rat-Man. For the Rat-Man's obsessional neurosis,
riddled with questions of guilt, remorse, and in-
debtedness, is a kind of matrix in which the problematic of the superego is treated before the term itself surfaces in Freud's writing. Now the key point is that the
concrete form in which the superego *enters* Freud's
thought is as the obscene rats which would *penetrate*
the anuses of those beloved by the Rat-Man were he
not to acquit himself of a thoroughly imaginary debt.
As the Rat-Man discloses his "great obsessive fear,"
Freud notes, his expression reveals what can only be
interpreted as "horror at pleasure of his own of which
he himself was unaware."[41] The upshot of Laplanche's
analysis is to relibidinize the concept of the superego:
"Le surmoi apparaît parfois comme un rat, jouisseur,
cruel, image même de la pulsion. De sorte que le conflit
moral, torturant, implacable, apparemment assimila-
ble à un conflit qui serait élevé, ne fait que recouvrir
une lutte 'cruelle et lubrique' où le châtiment suprême
est aggloméré toujours avec la jouissance suprême."[42]
The rats would function as phobic objects no longer

41. "Notes Upon a Case of Obsessional Neurosis" in *Three Case
Histories* (New York: Collier, 1963), p. 27.
42. Laplanche, *Bulletin de Psychologie,* No. 306 (1972–73), p. 728.

available to any disguise of their horrendously libidinal nature.

Victor Hugo? Let us recall the *scene* in which the *sum-bolon* is revealed in *Notre-Dame de Paris*. La Esmeralda draws her slipper from the *toque-sein* at the entry of the penitent's cave, "cavité noire, sombre et humide" (p. 154). Inscribed above is an edifying call to prayer and remorse: TU, ORA; whence the popular name for Gudule's retreat: "Trou aux rats." The introduction of the *symbolique* thus takes place within a duplicitous field of script, oscillating, beyond any possibility of synthesis, between the appeal to conscience of TU, ORA and its obscenely anal reinscription as "Trou aux rats." The *symbolique* enters Hugo's novel in exactly the same manner, through the very same orifice, as the superego penetrates into Freud's thought: midst excrement and puns. Puns, we recall: "la fiente de l'esprit qui vole." Consider the moves of our *tocsin,* the allegedly humble bearer of the Law. In *Quatrevingt-treize,* we found it ripping apart the acoustic circuit of mouth and ear. For La Esmeralda it became *toque-sein.* Now, with Gudule, it is anal. The circuit of the Law ("castration," the "symbolique") would seem to be indistinguishable from the possibilities of perversion itself.

III.

Laplanche's third incursion against the restrictive normativity of Oedipus and castration concerns the formation of the superego through parental identification. In the normal Oedipal situation, the boy, failing to attain his desired (maternal) object, renounces his desire and identifies with his father. Now ultimately, the only theory of identification concretely sustained by psychoanalytic practice concerns identification with the lost love object. But precisely to that extent Freud, in the third chapter of *The Ego and the Id,* is forced into the paradoxical affirmation that the "normal" identification runs contrary to "our expectation."[43] For according to the theory, the boy should end up identifying with his mother. Because of this dilemma, Freud seems almost relieved to encounter the negative or homosexual Oedipal position, for it would allow the boy to emerge from the Oedipal crisis with a "normal" paternal identification.

Laplanche's solution to the problem suggests that every Oedipus complex is both positive and negative, and that, paradoxically, it is the positive Oedipal position which results in a homosexual identification and the negative one which issues in a normal or heterosexual one. What such a chiasmatization of the Oedipus complex eliminates is any possibility of interpretation in terms of an apprenticeship in love. For the heavily normative trend in Freudian sexual theory is rooted in the ultimately behaviorist notion that one *learns* one's sexuality, for better or for worse, in the Oedipal moment, that one will love in perpetuity more or less as one has loved Oedipally. And with the idea of a sexuality that is learned comes the possibility of a failure to learn the lesson, of a botched apprenticeship. But in the model presented, one by no means learns one's sexuality; rather, one identifies— chiasmatically—into it. One will end up loving pre-

43. *The Ego and the Id* in the *Standard Edition,* vol. XIX, p. 32.

cisely as one *did not love* (predominantly) during the Oedipal moment. The question of Oedipal identification is opened to the freedom and rhetorical complexity of dream-work. As the behaviorist interpretation is dissolved, the entire problem of the resolution of the Oedipus complex invites reconceptualization in far less moralistic terms.

Consider now the conclusion of *Notre-Dame de Paris*. Claude Frollo, in his move to punish La Esmeralda, absents himself just long enough for the melodramatic reunion with Gudule to take place. That situation alone would confirm our interpretation of Cimourdain as mother at the end of *Quatrevingt-treize,* for it is as though the vindictive pair in the earlier novel were conflated in the later one: Cimourdain is a condensation of Claude Frollo and Gudule. Plainly, Hugo is drawing on identical imaginative resources in the conclusion of each novel. And to that extent, we may imagine a superimposition of the two as an intertextual entity possessing a certain autonomy and in itself worthy of consideration. But in that case, at the moment of the introduction of the *symbolique* (in *Notre-Dame de Paris*), we find the composite character La Esmeralda-Gauvain confronting the maternal-paternal-amorous-punitive instance Gudule-Frollo-Cimourdain. That is, our intertext would seem to offer every possibility of sexual identification, a matrix sufficiently complex to be open to just those chiasmatic effects posited by Laplanche in the case of Freud. Surely, with the infinitely perverse La Esmeralda at the heart of the action, one is not running too risky a wager in positing at least the virtuality of their occurrence.

The elaboration of our *tocsin,* we have suggested, has
been implicitly a reading of one of the most remarkable and demanding texts to have emerged from France
in recent years, Jacques Derrida's *Glas.* That implicit-
ness is perhaps worth respecting, since one is hard put
to imagine a metalanguage at present capable of explicitly *comprehending* that text. Still, a series of necessar-
ily schematic remarks on *Glas* may help to clarify its
relation to our own undertaking, and indeed bring into
better relief the analyses pursued above.

    1. *Glas* is first of all an effort at a materialist disman-
tling of the concept of sociality in Hegel. To that extent, it may be Derrida's *Marx,* a thinker whose texts
have never been engaged explicitly by Derrida, but
who haunts, at times more than allusively, many a
page of the Frenchman's text. Our own reading of
Marx, for instance, whose point of departure was
what Marx called an "uncanny anonymity," might
well be regarded as a commentary on the following
passage: "on ne touche pas au glas, donc, sans toucher
à la classe. Mais le discours codé, policé sur la lutte des
classes, s'il forclôt la question du glas (tout ce qui s'y
forge, tout ce sur quoi elle retentit, en particulier l'ex-
propriation du nom partout où elle porte) manque au
moins une révolution. Et qu'est-ce qu'une révolution
qui ne s'attaque pas au nom propre" (p. 232).[44]

    2. Now the concept of sociality deconstructed by
Derrida is above all that of the family. For his analysis
is directed at both the concept of the family and a
certain familialism of the concept, at that level of

----

44. Page references in the text are to *Glas* (Paris: Galilée, 1974).

Hegel's discourse at which "l'ontologie ne se laisse plus décoller du familial" (p. 67). Indeed, the Marxian title that recurs most often in *Glas* is *The Holy Family*. But the attack on Hegel's "family" soon takes the form of a dismantling of the Freudian concept of castration: "Je l'ai toujours dit, répondrait Hegel aux docteurs de la castration" (p. 52). It is worth noting that what we have called Derrida's *Marx* should take the odd form of a reading of Freud. For one suspects that at this juncture in the history of reading, the interpretative medium within and against which the most radical moves may be effected is the works of Freud. (It was for that reason that our own reading of Marx turned on the death drive; our reading of Hugo on a dismantling of castration.) In Derrida's case, the unhinging of "castration" works against that erotico-philosophical matrix in which, "l'*Aufhebung,* concept central de la relation sexuelle, articule le phallocentrisme le plus traditionnel sur l'onto-théo-téléologie hegelienne" (p. 130). The erotics eventually *affirmed* in the text posit a plurality of sexual differences in opposition to *the* difference between the sexes. What is effected is a reinscription of Oedipus in which it would be possible to occupy all positions simultaneously (p. 203).

3. The structure of Derrida's dismantling consists in actively *losing* Hegel's text in that of Jean Genet, most particularly in *Notre-Dame des Fleurs.* Whence the typographical oddity of the book: a column on Hegel set against a column on Genet. *Glas,* then, would disperse the construct of metaphysics in a poetico-erotic thieves' carnival of perversity, a world of *argot.* We need only allude here to the philosopher Gringoire lost

in the Cour des Miracles: "Me voilà donc en habit
d'histrion, comme saint Genest. Que voulez-vous?
c'est une éclipse" (p. 185).

4. The movement by which the dialectics of Hegel
are lost in the "galactics" of Genet is assimilated by
Derrida to that of a silent bell, a written text: "entre les
deux, le battant d'un autre texte, on dirait d'une autre logique!"[45] (Recall the entry of Gringoire into the
Cour des Miracles, of Lantenac into the Vendée.) The
movement of *Glas* is that of writing as *tocsin/toc-seing*:
"Il rejoue la mimesis et l'arbitraire de la signature dans
un accouplement déchaîné (toc/seing/lait), ivre comme
un sonneur à sa corde pendue."[46] We are approaching
La Esmeralda, our *toque-sein,* here: "Le glas tinte à
proximité de la tétine"; "quelle forme lactifère reconnaître au tocsin?" (pp. 172–73).

5. The two other principal media through which
Derrida's disarticulation of castration is pursued are
plants *(Notre-Dame de Fleurs)* and minerals. "Ce discours sur la différence sexuelle . . . exclut les plantes"
(p. 131). "Au programme depuis toujours . . . , l'an-
thoedipe arrive à chaque saison comme une fleur"
(p. 200). La Esmeralda, a writing machine containing
a *symbolique* which it exceeds: a heliotrope. As for minerals, as matter itself, they constitute the resistance of
materialism, above all, perhaps, to the ideality of a
certain interiority of sound: "Le son qu'il [le minéral]
émet lorsqu'il est frappé, il ne l'émet pas de lui-même,
comme une voix, mais il le reçoit comme d'une source
étrangère" (p. 119). La Esmeralda, the false name, the
green stone: heliotrope.

45. *Glas,* "Prière d'insérer."
46. *Ibid.*

6. *Glas* is studded with neologisms. Derrida: "J'ar-gotise, je jargonne, j'ai l'air de produire des mots nouveaux, un nouveau lexique. Un argot seulement, un jargon" (p. 246). The reader may be reminded here of our reinscriptions of *tocsin (toque-sein, toc-seing,* etc.). A word of amplification may be of help at this juncture. What is offensive about such a procedure, I suspect, is the clarity with which it betrays the violence of interpretative activity. For we persist in regarding texts as monuments which must not be defaced. And yet the model of reading that has oriented the analyses above, and that has guided Derrida's efforts in *Glas* as well, I believe, would see in a text the point of intersec-tion of a number of interpretative forces. A text is less a monument than a battlefield. The interpreter's task, then, is to situate his own efforts strategically at the crux of that struggle and to ally himself with that stratum of the text generative of the greatest intensity. But to the extent that one has been able to work within the node or matrix of the various forces, the pursuit of the "battle" will take the form of a rigorous positing of the lines along which and the conditions under which the work may be *rewritten*. It is that process of rewrit-ing the language—of the text—that is referred to in Derrida's affirmation: "j'argotise."

> Sei ein klingendes Glas,
> das sich im Klang schon zerschlug.
> —RILKE

Victor Hugo's *Glas*? The element within which to think through our own modernity? The suggestion seems ludicrous. Yet however outrageous, it is hardly

original; it is indeed the organizing subtext of Mallarmé's important essay, *Crise de vers*. That text deals
with the fallout of a specific event, the death of Victor
Hugo. "Un lecteur français, ses habitudes inter-
rompues à la mort de Victor Hugo, ne peut que se
déconcerter" (p. 360).[47] Hugo's accomplishment had
been in reducing all discursive forms to the line of
verse: "Hugo, dans sa tâche mystérieuse, rabattit toute
la prose, philosophie, éloquence, histoire au vers, et
comme il était le vers personnellement, il confisque
chez qui pense, discourt ou narre, presque le droit à
s'énoncer" (p. 361). Meanwhile, as though uncon-
sciously, within the language, a shattering of Hugo's
hegemony was silently in preparation: "Le vers, je
crois, avec respect attendit que le géant qui l'identifiait
à sa main tenace et plus ferme toujours de forgeron,
vînt à manquer; pour, lui, se rompre" (p. 361). The
break up of the classical line of verse, a new poetic
mobility, was concomitant with Hugo's death, and
our modernity—"Jugez le goût très moderne"—is nothing but that dispersion.

From the meditation that follows we shall cite two
exquisite formulations of the new esthetic. The first
concerns the disappearance of the poetic voice within
the differential medium of the poem:

L'oeuvre pure implique la disparition élocutoire du poète,
qui cède l'initiative aux mots, par le heurt de leur inégalité
mobilisés; ils s'allument de reflets réciproques comme une
virtuelle traînée de feux sur des pierreries, remplaçant la
respiration perceptible en l'ancien souffle lyrique ou la direction personnelle enthousiaste de la phrase. (p. 366)

47. Page references in the text are to *Crise de vers* in *Oeuvres
complètes* (Paris: Pléiade, 1945).

"Hugo's death" would seem, then, to be reinscribed in this passage as a more general structure of literary "experience." To *write,* for Mallarmé, would seem to be to reenact that erosion of the "pneumatics" of poetry of which Hugo was a prime practitioner. Writing is tantamount to repeating the death of Hugo.

The second passage posits a certain intertextuality through which a poem's mode of existence might be its relation to another poem:

Quelque symétrie, parallèlement, qui, de la situation des vers en la pièce se lie à l'authenticité de la pièce dans le volume, vole, outre le volume, à plusieurs inscrivant, eux, sur l'espace spirituel, le paraphe amplifié du génie, anonyme et parfait comme une existence d'art. (p. 367)

Poetry becomes the anonymous medium corrosive of authorial identity and of that idea of closure without which the book as institution is unthinkable.

Consider now the apparently insignificant circumstances in which Mallarmé pursues his meditation. Of a rainy afternoon, the poet observes a certain reflection of the raindrops outside on the gloss of the binding of the works of his library:

Tout à l'heure, en abandon de geste, avec la lassitude que cause le mauvais temps désespérant une après l'autre l'après-midi, je fis retomber, sans une curiosité mais ce lui semble avoir lu tout voici vingt ans, l'effilé de multicolores perles qui plaque la pluie, encore, au chatoiement des brochures dans la bibliothèque. Maint ouvrage, sous la verroterie du rideau, alignera sa propre scintillation: j'aime comme en le ciel mûr, contre la vitre, à suivre des lueurs d'orage. (p. 360)

The raindrops are metaphorized as jewels ("perles"), then as false jewels or glassbeads ("verroterie"). That

glass, however, is itself behind glass ("vitre"), and that
already complicated vibration of glass against glass
functions as a parasitical reflection on the gloss of the
works in the library. "Effilé" comes from the verb for
unraveling (*effiler*). That unraveling, then, is being
exercised against the stitching ("brochures") of the
book bindings. The metaphorical play of the *verroterie*
would seem to be accomplishing that bursting of the
binding which was the task of the poetic revolution
referred to by Mallarmé in the passage cited above.

That revolution was epitomized by Mallarmé as the
break up of *le vers*. That division, we now sense, is
doubly inscribed. Its first sense is the emergence of
"free verse." But its second, operated by the text, is the
silent split between *vers* and *verre*. For in a somewhat
hallucinatory manner, it is the *verroterie* that seems to
elude the very dimension of the text's meaning in
order to perform within the text what is presented as a
literary program pursued by others. At this point, we
would invoke Mallarmé's reference to the differential
medium in which the "pneumatics" of poetry come to
grief: "une virtuelle traînée de feux sur des pierreries"
(p. 366). For our *verroterie,* our glass behind glass, is
metaphorized as a series of jewels (*perles*). Once again,
literary modernity would seem to come into existence
within the metaphoricity of *verre*.

The "majestic unconscious idea" whose fruition the
text announces is that literature itself is indistinguishable from poetry: "que la forme appellée vers est sim-
plement elle-même la littérature" (p. 361). But within
the text, *vers* itself, in its operations, is indistinguishable from a certain play of *verr(oterie)*. This vitrification

of literature is also known as the (interminable) death of Victor Hugo. Now given this interplay between glass and the demise of the great man, can one fail to detect within this essay by the author of *Les Mots anglais* the word *glas (de Victor Hugo)*? *Crise de vers*: "le vers qui de plusieurs vocables refait un mot total, neuf, étranger à la langue et comme incantatoire . . ." (p. 368). *Glas*: "commentaire du mot absent qu'il dé-limite, enveloppe, sert, entoure de ses soins. Le texte *se présente* comme le métalangage du langage qui ne se présente pas" (p. 148). Somewhere between French and English, from German if one likes, Mallarmé has us inscribe a "new word"—*Glas(s)*—in the language, in his text. *Il argotise*. *Verroterie/vers; verroterie verte*: Mallarmé's text stutters *virtually* the same sequence as La Esmeralda explaining her name. Each repetition of an all but silent difference serves as the means through which a book comes undone, unbound.[48] Plainly, within the network allowing us to observe Mallarmé literally repeating that stratum of Hugo's work re-peated in Derrida's *Glas,* any reference to an "anxiety of influence" is beside the point. For how can the very concept of priority survive in a web in which our *tocsin (toque-sein),* the precursor of danger, is made of

48. "Pour les écrivains du début de ce siècle, rien ne paraissait aussi différent qu'Hugo et Mallarmé. La plupart de nos parents ou grands-parents, s'ils connaissaient les deux, s'imaginaient qu'on ne pouvait les aimer à la fois. Peu à peu, l'éloignement nous permet d'apprécier leurs profondes affinités, et bientôt il deviendra évident pour tous que l'on ne peut vraiment comprendre l'un sans l'autre." Michel Butor, "Victor Hugo romancier" in *Répertoire* (Paris: Minuit, 1960), p. 242.

glas(s)—*verroterie*—the very matter of ulteriority. As for "anxiety," we have seen how the very concept, in its strongest formulation (Freud), is disarticulated by a certain duplicity of the tocsin (toxin). A step further, and what will be disoriented is the interpretative will to truth itself. For given the metaphorico-metonymical chain: *verroterie-verte-vers-vitre-virtuelle,* how sure can one be that *vérité* itself has remained uncontaminated?

As our glassbead game proliferates, diminishing ever more in transcendence, in any possibility of mastery, we may wonder where indeed we have been taken. We have seen Mallarmé's esthetic fly literally . . . out the window in the very words through which it was articulated. Similarly, Hugo's classical evocation of a cathedral was seen to be simultaneously at work at its erosion. More strangely still, both these movements seemed traceable, indifferently, to the writing machine of Hugo's novel of 1793. Hugo-Mallarmé? Hugo-Derrida? In what element are we moving? What critical monstrosity have we wrought?

In an effort to gain some insight into the functioning of our own analysis, to discover our bearings, we shall turn to that bastion of strength in Hugo's *oeuvre,* Jean Valjean. Our point of departure, however, shall be the admission that as *character,* Jean Valjean is a fundamentally rotten construct. For his situation in the novel is that of the poor man . . . who happens to have a fortune. Hugo would have him blessed with all the virtues of the impoverished and yet simultaneously capable of buying and selling anyone in the text . . . which, in order to obtain custody of Cosette, he does. He is what Sartre would call a "non-synthetic unification," as Cosette herself blurts out in a moment of naive enthusiasm: "qu'il donnait beaucoup aux pauvres, mais qu'il était pauvre lui-même."[49] Jean Valjean: *le misérable* as millionaire.

The question then becomes: where does he derive his money from? More generally: what is the *economy* within which the contradictory pathos of Jean Valjean may function? That key question is disposed of, in this novel of 1500 pages, in a chapter a single page in length. Its title: "Histoire d'un progrès dans les ver-roteries noires" ("Premiere partie, Livre cinquième, I"):

De temps immémorial, M.—sur M—avait pour industrie spéciale l'imitation des jais anglais et des verroteries noires d'Allemagne. Cette industrie avait toujours végété, à cause de la cherté des matières premières qui réagissait sur la main d'oeuvre. Au moment où Fantine revint à M.—sur M—, une transformation inouïe s'était opérée dans cette produc-tion des "articles noirs." Vers la fin de 1815, un homme, un inconnu, était venu s'établir dans la ville et avait eu l'idée de substituer, dans cette fabrication, la gomme-lacque à la ré-sine et, pour les bracelets en particulier, les coulants en tôle soudée.

Ce tout petit changement en effet avait prodigieusement réduit le prix de la matière première, ce qui avait permis, premièrement, d'élever le prix de la main-d'oeuvre, bien-fait pour le pays, deuxièmement d'améliorer la fabrication, avantage pour le consommateur, troisièmement de vendre à meilleur marché tout en triplant le bénéfice, profit pour le manufacturier.

Ainsi pour une idée trois résultats.[50]

49. *Oeuvres complètes,* vol. X, p. 716.
50. *Ibid.,* p. 161.

Tres para una. The magnificent idea, the "unheard of"—or silent—"transformation," takes on all the prestige of a Hugolian heroine. And what is that idea except the introduction of a substitute ("la gomme-lacque") into an imitation of what is essentially an imitation ("verroterie") of a jewel? Like La Esmeralda, that other creature of "glass," the *verroterie* of Jean Valjean would seem to be metaphorical in its essence: the imitation of an imitation of an imitation.

There remains, of course, a final bit of substitutive trickery inseparable from the very mode of existence of the glassbeads of *Les Misérables*: the surplus-value extorted in the course of their production. It is a deception whose first dupe was no doubt Hugo himself, blinded in his enthusiasm for the humanitarian industrialist.[51] And yet it is precisely that invisible supplement, the surplus-value drawn from a glassworks, that provides the very medium in which the pathos of Jean Valjean—that is, of Victor Hugo—becomes possible.

In our efforts to constitute the rudiments of a general economy of Hugo's novels, have we done anything else than render explicit the process through which surplus-value may be drawn from the production of *verroterie*? As the *verroterie verte* of La Esmeralda became disseminated through and beyond the novels of Hugo, we saw it fission into *toque-sein, toc-seing, tocsin, vers* and *glas*. It is just that endlessly generative capacity to be worth *more* than the author's—or reader's—in-

51. See Joan W. Scott, *The Glassworkers of Carmaux: French Craftsmen and Political Action in a Nineteenth-Century City* (Cambridge: Harvard, 1974) for a discussion of just how exploitative glassworks such as that of "Monsieur Madeleine" actually were.

tentionality seems willing to pay for it that has fasci-
nated us in Hugo, and it is the surprising systematicity
through which it may nevertheless be detected that
has formed the object of our analysis.[52]

The classical Marxist will object at this point that our
invocation of the concept of surplus-value is superficial, willfully perverse. But for a certain Marxism, to
write within the problematic of Hugo is inevitably to
fall prey to a debilitating relation to surfaces. Lukacs is
exemplary here. Toward the end of his history of the
decline of the French novel after Balzac, he berates
Zola for a failure to seize human reality from *within*.
His novels' magnificent evocations are limited to "the
outer trappings."[53] But soon Zola's particular vice
comes to be crystallized around the name of its practitioner *par excellence*: "Hence, as soon as Zola departs
from the monotony of naturalism, he is immediately
transmuted into a decorative picturesque romanticist,
who treads in the footsteps of Victor Hugo with his
bombastic monumentalism. There is a strange element
of tragedy here."[54] "Victor Hugo" is, then, the name
of an ideal type: the risk run by imagination that it be
diverted from a centralizing perception of human reality to thoroughly secondary concerns, to mere
"backdrop." As such, the Hugolian tendency is fun-

52. See the appendix to this volume for a consideration of the
place of the two great novels of Hugo that we have not
discussed—*L'Homme qui rit* and *Les Travailleurs de la mer*—within
our general economy.

53. *Studies in European Realism* (New York: Grosset and Dunlap,
1964), p. 92.

54. *Ibid.*, p. 93.

damentally opposed to the Marxist orientation. For
what, according to Lukacs, is the distinguishing attri-
bute of the Marxist? "Marxists look for the true high-
road of history, the true direction of its development,
the true course of the historical curve, the formula of
which they know; and because they know the formula
they do not fly off at a tangent at every hump in the
graph . . . . "[55] The Marxist is, then, opposed to the
Hugolian as center is to tangent, as the essential is to
the accidental.

But at this juncture we would pause to observe how
little that evocation of the "Marxist" perception of
history agrees with our own examination of Marx's
delineation of French history. For the medium within
which that history functioned was one of an endless
proliferation of tangents. Farce marked a deviation
from the dialectical pair of tragedy and comedy. The
lumpen-proletariat could rise to the top of the social
structure, and exercise Marx's fascination as it did,
only in a world in which "the true course of the historical curve," the movement of dialectic itself, was seen
to skid off course. To choose a final example, the intended progress within Marx's discourse from a deluded notion of representation (the state as representative of the whole of society) to a true notion (the state as
representative of a single exploitative class) gave way
with "Bonapartism" to a state *in opposition to* society
and consequently representing no class at all. In every
instance, the movement of Marx's text is affirmative of
the tangent. It was at this stage of our analysis,

55. *Ibid.*, p. 5.

moreover, that we had occasion to invoke Marx's references to Hugo, whom he regarded as unduly respectful of the representational model. For whereas Hugo played Napoléon le Petit off against Napoléon le Grand, Marx suggested that the real significance of the later figure was to demonstrate the profound pettiness of the allegedly Great Napoleon. Which is to say that Hugo's formulation was insufficiently corrosive of the center. Marx is to Hugo as an affirmation of an irreducible tangent is to that of the center.

Need we say that our reading of Hugo was in many ways an effort to open his texts up to the kind of radical *excess* we detected in Marx? Our *tocsin* functions within Hugo much as "Bonapartism" does in Marx. Our proto-text in *Quatrevingt-treize,* in fact, a shattering cry within a ramifying field of script, affirmed what Lukacs calls the "backdrop" at the expense of "the event in all its human import." Similarly our textual *theoria* in *Notre-Dame de Paris* was resolutely and perversely superficial, even as our reading of *Crise de vers* delineated within that text a surprising centrality of "the external setting." In brief, we are making two claims. The first is that there is nothing less "Marxist," in the sense given that term by Lukacs in the passage quoted, than the texts of Marx we examined. The second is that a certain superficiality, an uncannily perverse combination of rigor and flimsiness is the very element within which those texts effect their strongest moves. To work, as we have attempted, in a significant relation to those texts is inevitably to move within the dimension castigated by Lukacs as being "tangential."

Our reading of Hugo, then, has endeavored to coin-

cide with what might be termed a stratum of originary
deviance within the writings of an author who, for
Lukacs, constitutes the deviation *par excellence* from
the "classical tradition." For the choice before Zola,
according to the Marxist, was either to rediscover the
sources of his art in Balzac or to exacerbate his pen-
chant for the external and emerge an epigone of Hugo.
In its purest state, the opposition between Balzac and
Zola gives way to one between Balzac and Hugo, and
Lukacs all but concludes his strange effort to merge the
preservation of classical tradition with the pursuit of
class struggle by quoting a letter from the aging
Goethe in which he judges quite severely *Notre-Dame
de Paris* in relation to *La Peau de chagrin*. For that reason,
we shall conclude our analysis by turning briefly to
that interpretative tendency which functions as a pressure to inhibit the kind of reading we have undertaken,
to exclude that articulation between Marx's writings
and the literature of the nineteenth century whose matrix we have begun to delineate. Its most general name
in Lukacs is "Balzac's realism."

For reasons soon to be made clear, the text we shall
consider is *Les Chouans*. It is the first novel signed
Balzac and as such may perhaps be regarded as a
metonym—or emblem—of French "realism" itself.
What follows, it should be emphasized, is less a reading
of Balzac's novel than a sorting out of various components of an interpretative possibility opened up by the
text and grouped under the generic term "realism."

If we have chosen *Les Chouans,* it is because it brings
us conveniently back to our point of departure, the
counter-revolution in the West of France. But the

novel's subtitle is *La Bretagne en 1799*. Six years after 1793, we are in a degraded phase of the struggle. Counter-revolutionary violence is perpetually degenerating into sheer banditry. Property, rather than law, is the focus of this new defiance. As for the Republic, its spiritual and physical bankruptcy are everywhere apparent in this year of the 18 Brumaire. Consider the comparison with *Quatrevingt-treize*. Instead of sending out a dashing young aristocrat (Gauvain) to quell the opposition, the Republic, in Balzac's novel, commissions a high-class courtesan (Marie de Verneuil), the former mistress of the fallen Danton, to seduce the leader of the counter-revolution. Her chief rival for his affections is the former mistress of the legendary leader of the Vendée, Charette. In place of Hugo's fanatical Jacobin Cimourdain, we find as *délégué civil* in Balzac the somewhat creepy and venal police spy in Fouché's employ, Corentin.[56] In brief, the situation in Balzac is one of generalized belatedness functioning implicitly in the service of demystificatory irony.

56. The central chapter in *Les Chouans* is called "Une Idée de Fouché." The changed situation of Fouché, Jacobin terrorist in 1793 become Napoleonic Minister of Police, captures nicely the shift in the six years separating the action of Hugo's novel from that of Balzac's. Consider Fouché's admonitions to Bernadotte, the Minister of War, just prior to the 18 Brumaire: "Imbécile! où vas-tu et que veux-tu faire? En 93, à la bonne heure, il y avait tout à gagner, à defaire et à refaire . . . . Puisque nous voilà arrivés et que nous n'avons plus qu'à perdre, pourquoi continuer?" (F. Furet and D. Richet, *La Révolution française* [Paris: Fayard, 1973], p. 484). On the side of the revolution, as with the Chouans, a cynical regard for property is the overriding concern.

The reader has already intuited that in *Les Chouans,*
Balzac has served us his reading of the myth of Judith,
and Marie de Verneuil is on more than one occasion
castigated by her adversaries as "une Judith des rues"
(p. 173).[57] But such an introduction of sexual intrigue
into the political brings us to a second important component in the interpretative complex we are delineating: the psychologization of the historical action. For
there is an undeniable pressure in the text on the part of
both Balzac and his characters to transform the
historical-political drama into a love story interpretable in terms of individual passions. Marie de Verneuil
gives most blatant expression to this tendency. Upon
discovery of her would-be lover's apparent treachery,
her great fear is that the action of the novel exceed the
psychological: "mais le rebelle mourra donc pour
avoir porté des armes contre son pays? La France me
volerait donc ma vengeance! . . . que rien ne trahisse
ma trahison . . . " (p. 213). It will be noted that to the
extent that passion reaches that pitch of intensity allowing it to claim for its own the action of the novel, it
is in the specific form of ambivalence: Marie discovers
her hatred for the man she loves. That psychological
insight is formulated with maximal explicitness by
Corentin, the agent of the police, in discussion with the
revolutionary captain Hulot:

—Mais elle ne nous le livrera jamais, ajouta-t-il [Hulot]
en hochant la tete.
—Oh! si! répliqua Corentin.
—Ne voyez-vous pas qu'elle l'aime? reprit Hulot.
—C'est précisément pour cela. (p. 214)

57. Page references in the text are to *Les Chouans* (Paris: Livre de
Poche, 1972).

In *Quatrevingt-treize,* passion at its most intense was free from ambivalence: Michelle Fléchard's maternal love.[58] The conflicts were ethical. In Balzac's novel of 1799, then, we find a psychology sufficiently complex to emerge as central to the action. We are, no doubt, approaching here what Lukacs calls "the adequate presentation of the complete human personality."[59] Within the novel, that psychology—of ambivalence —is part of the tactical expertise of the police.

A third dimension of our interpretative complex is what might be termed "realism" in the restricted sense, that ability to *see* social reality despite one's preconceptions. There is an elaborate morality of vision which Lukacs, drawing on Engels, affirms in his analysis of Balzac.[60] *To see* is the honorific verb *par excellence* in *Studies in European Realism.* Now within the novel, Marie comes to understand the war in the West in a flash of vision. What she observes is the series of earthern walls isolating every peasant enclosure from the

58. In the one novel in which Hugo shows himself to be a master analyst of psychological ambivalence and eccentricity, *L'Homme qui rit,* one has the feeling that such analysis is there almost as part of the local color, as though "Psychology" were the name of a refrain one hummed when in England.

59. *Studies in European Realism,* p. 7.

60. "That Balzac thus was compelled to go against his own class sympathies and political prejudices, that he *saw* the necessity of the downfall of his favorite nobles, and described them as people deserving not better fate; and that he *saw* the real men of the future where, for the time being, they alone were to be found—that I consider one of the grandest triumphs of Realism, and one of the grandest features of old Balzac." Engels, from the draft of a letter to Margaret Harkness, Beginning of April, 1888. Marx and Engels, *On Literature and Art,* ed. L. Baxandall and S. Morawski (Saint Louis: Telos Press, 1973), p. 116.

next: "Ces haies et ces échaliers donnent au sol la physionomie d'un immense échiquier dont chaque champ forme une case parfaitement isolée des autres, close comme une forteresse, protégée comme elle par des remparts" (p. 276). It is these multiple divisions of the terrain which render the region untakable by a regular army: "Là était tout le secret de la guerre des Chouans. Mademoiselle de Verneuil comprit alors la nécessité où se trouvait la République d'étouffer la discorde plutôt par des moyens de police et de diplomatie que par l'inutile emploi de la force militaire" (p. 277). Again, the contrast with the situation in Hugo's novel is worth noting. The peasant West in *Quatrevingt-treize* was an infinitely subtle subterranean system of communication. In *Les Chouans,* we find a series of irreducibly isolated units. We find, then, in Balzac a physical situation identical to that of the "paysans parcellaires" in *The Eighteenth Brumaire of Louis Bonaparte.* What Marie *sees* is a graphic illustration of Marx's evocation of peasant isolation in that text: "Their mode of production isolates them from one another instead of bringing them into mutual intercourse . . . ."[61] Shall we suggest that Balzac's "realism" consists in his ability to afford illustrations of Marx's theory? Lukacs does as much in his discussion of *Les Paysans*: "Balzac here gives us a masterly picture of the peasant smallholding. He describes what Marx, in *The Eighteenth Brumaire,* formulates theoretically as the essence of the development of smallholding after the French Revolution."[62] Balzac's realism would thus amount to a ca-

61. *Der Achtzehnte Brumaire,* p. 117.
62. *Studies in European Realism,* p. 35.

pacity for *seeing* the reality formulated theoretically by Marx. But within the novel, what Marie comes to see is a certain relation between autonomous social units and the imperative of the police.

In this first novel signed Balzac, we have come to isolate the components of an interpretative complex: demystificatory irony; refined analysis of individual motivation; acute *perception* of social reality. But in each case, the novel thematized each element in relation to the newly emergent force of the police. The degradation of counter-revolutionary violence was toward common thievery. A psychology of ambivalence was one of the exemplary disciplines mastered by Corentin. What Balzac *saw*—through Marie's eyes—as the secret of the historical drama amounted to an intuition of the necessity of the police. It is in this context that we would insist on Balzac's clear implication that the man of the future in France is Corentin. Whereas in *Quatrevingt-treize,* it is Gauvain, the military hero, who represents the future in relation to Cimourdain, in *Les Chouans,* the honorable and aged revolutionary soldier Hulot is dismissed by the surprisingly young police spy at the novel's end: "—Voilà encore un de mes honnêtes gens qui ne feront jamais fortune, se dit Corentin quand il fut loin du corps de garde" (p. 401).

One might, of course, reduce this last opposition to one between *genres*: Hugo's romance/Balzac's novel. But surely the *text* of Hugo that we came to discover is by no means described by that generic term. Consider two propositions. On the basis of a reading of *Les Chouans,* we may well agree with Lukacs that the fu-

ture of the novel is with that excellence of *vision* which
is the distinguishing mark of "realism." But simultaneously, we would affirm that the novel leads us to
the conclusion that the future of France is with the
police. We are suggesting here the existence of what
might be called, in Michel Foucault's terms, an
"epistemologico-juridical formation."[63] This is not
the place to discuss Foucault's magnificent analyses of
the origin of prisons. And yet if he is correct in positing
a politics implicit in the very discursiveness of every
form of knowledge; and if we may accept his suggestion that the very epistemophilic passion to *see* or
examine human reality, which orients our human sci-
ences, is shot through with a fantasy of surveillance,
then we shall have located a politico-literary point of
intersection between the "future of the novel" and the
"future of France" evoked above. The interpretative
tendency culminating in Lukacs' morality of vision
would be irrevocably contaminated by Corentin's
dream of surveillance. Together they would contrib-
ute to an interpretation of "the nineteenth century"
against which the present work has been written.[64]

63. *Surveiller et punir: Naissance de la prison* (Paris: Gallimard,
1975), p. 28.
64. Having brought this chapter back to its place of origin—the
counter-revolution in the West of France—we are inclined to move
the analysis still forward in time, still backward in these pages to
the opening of our book: the (second) Eighteenth Brumaire. In
view of the failure of prisons, from their very inception, to accomplish their alleged aims, Foucault asks the probing question:
what purpose is served by the failure of prisons? His answer: the
assurance of a highly visible ("voyant") restricted economy of
"delinquents," of cops and robbers, within the more general
economy of illegality constitutive of society. That restricted

economy, we would suggest, reaches its perfection once "criminals" and police enter into explicit complicity, for cops and robbers then emerge in their full specularity. Foucault: "Il semble qu'en France, ce soit autour de la Révolution de 1848 et de la prise de pouvoir de Louis-Napoléon que ces pratiques aient atteint leur plein épanouissement." (*Ibid.*, p. 286.) In a footnote, the author refers his reader to that very evocation of the Society of December 10 in *The Eighteenth Brumaire* that allowed us, at the beginning of this work, to begin the construction of what we called a "general economy" of Marx's delineation of French history. Restricted economy/general economy? Literature/History? May this concluding footnote to a footnote in Foucault's text serve as an indication of the Möbian topology within which such questions are to be thought.

Appendix

What follows are the elements of an interpretation of the two major novels of Hugo that we have not referred to in the body of the text: *L'Homme qui rit* and *Les Travailleurs de la mer*. These readings are intended specifically to demonstrate the insertion of both books in the general economy of Hugo's novels we have constructed.

I.

L'Homme qui rit is the story of the failed conversion of Gwynplaine, the disfigured histrion, become Lord Clancharlie, member of the House of Lords. The measure of that failure is the hysterical laughter he provokes in the House when his grin breaks out in the course of his maiden speech. For that laughter *repeats* the reaction of his audiences in the "Green-Box" performances of *Le Chaos vaincu*. The coveted change is eroded by a more fundamental repetition.

But what are the ingredients of the desired conversion? In acceding to his origin, Gwynplaine would simultaneously discover his *voice,* the special eloquence which would allow him to speak the truth (of Hugo's humanitarianism) to those in power. The experience of conversion entails aspiring to a *politics of conversion* that is not without relation to the transfiguring experience of Lantenac upon hearing Michelle Fléchard's voice. (Like Gwynplaine, Michelle might say: "Moi, je ne suis rien, qu'une voix . . . .")[1] Note that the contradiction constitutive of Jean Valjean, the *misérable* as millionaire, is as well at the heart of Gwynplaine's new identity: "Je serai le lord des pauvres" (p. 402).

The originary truth of Gwynplaine's identity is discovered in a glass container abandoned at sea, "la gourde goudronnée que son enveloppe d'osier soutenait" (p. 109). The *gourde goudronnée* is superimposable on the *verroterie verte* of *Notre-Dame de Paris*. (The bottle containing Gwynplaine's identity is a version of the bottle—or imitation breast: *sein en toc*—whose milk keeps the infant Dea alive.) Laced into the wickerwork of the *gourde* is the name of the artist, Hardquanonne, who performed the disfiguring operation on Gwynplaine. The experience of the conversion is, then, as well, a journey to the "origin of the work of art," *Gwynplaine*. At that origin one finds a unique surgical practice, technically termed "*bucca fissa usque ad aures* (p. 266). That is, at the origin of Gwynplaine's authentically regained *voice* one finds a grotesque *parody* of the logocentric circuit of *mouth to ear*. It is as though that operation figured a logocentrism *sans réserve,* the very element of ideality pressed to such an extreme that it comes to be inscribed (*fissa,* split)

1. Page references in the text are to vol. XIV of Hugo, *Oeuvres complètes*.

grotesquely in the flesh—or matter—of Gwynplaine's face. At the origin of voice, then, there is a devastating inscription.

When Hardquanonne, the artist, is confronted with his masterwork in the torture chamber, he expends his last energy and dies—laughing. His crime, the buying and selling of a child, is known technically as *plagiarism: "Qui pueros vendis, plagiarius est tibi nomen"* (p. 268). At the origin of the work of art, then, is an incriminating act of perverse repetition or plagiarism: the parent loses his child; the artist dies laughing upon seeing his work.

The ceremonial of Gwynplaine's imagined conversion to Lord Clancharlie, the metaphorical "death of Gwynplaine," is witnessed by Ursus in a chapter entitled "Moenibus surdis campana muta." A death knell ("glas") rings too often to be the sound of a clock, and somehow escapes from time. In so doing, it seems to aspire to silence: "Toute prison autrefois, comme tout monastère, avait sa cloche dite muta, réservée aux occasions mélancoliques. La muta, 'la muette,' était une cloche tintant très bas, qui avait l'air de faire son possible pour n'être pas entendue" (p. 297). This evasion from temporality and sonority is a transition to the spatiality of a silent form of writing: "Un glas fait dans l'espace une vilaine ponctuation. Il marque, dans les préoccupations de tout le monde, des alinéas funèbres" (p. 298). We recognize the *tocsin* of *Quatrevingt-treize* here: the bell as silent writing machine which disarticulates the acoustic in the very movement through which it produces it.

II.

In *Les Travailleurs de la mer,* as in *L'Homme qui rit,* the action hinges on the retrieval of an object lost at sea: not the "jetsom" of the *gourde goudronnée,* but the "épave" of the steamship Durande, and specifically its "machine." If Gilliatt can rescue the engine from the shipwreck, he will win the hand of the woman he loves, the shipowner's "daughter"—actually his niece—Déruchette. Gilliatt, "homme du songe, pensif," sets out toward the reef in his boat, known in the novel by the archaic term, "panse."[2] At low tide, he discovers the wreck of the ship wedged in between the two "colonnes noires" or stony pillars of the reef known as the Douvres: "L'espèce d'immense *H* majuscule formé par les deux Douvres ayant la Durande pour trait d'union apparaissait à l'horizon dans on ne sait quelle majesté crépusculaire" (p. 670). This remarkable *H,* somewhere between nature (reef) and culture (machine), lost at sea, is, of course, the initial of Hugo (and of the artist Hardquanonne in *L'Homme qui rit*). A large part of the novel's action will consist in dismantling that signature.

Gilliatt's operation begins with him swinging by a rope from one column to the other of this magisterial *H*: "Franchir, pendu à ce fil, l'intervalle des deux Douvres; telle était la question" (p. 681). Gilliatt is here plainly in the role of Quasimodo in *Notre-Dame de Paris* (or of Jacques Derrida in *Glas*). This colossal form of writing is, then, at some level, as well, a bell. He next

2. Page references in the text are to vol. XII of Hugo, *Oeuvres complètes.*

builds a forge—"une espèce de poumon"—with hammer and anvil within a fissure of the reef (p. 688). The logocentric circuit of mouth (or lung) and ear (hammer and anvil) is literally inscribed within the letter *H*. He then proceeds to the surgical operation of castration, dislodging the precious machine, later to be turned in for the girl, from between the "jambages" of the letter *H* (p. 670). We may evoke the drama of that operation by indicating that Gilliatt, fending off the tempest from atop the reef in order to protect the "machine," repeats the episode of Quasimodo, fending off the *truands* from atop Notre-Dame de Paris in order to protect La Esmeralda. La Esmeralda as (writing) machine: we see how apt that assimilation was in our earlier analysis. *Verroterie* as a source of surplus-value: the unpaid labors of Gilliatt will restore to Mess Lethierry his wealth.

When Gilliatt finally succeeds in lodging the machine in his boat and in returning home to Guernesey, his intention, of course, is to trade in what Lacan would call "the signifier of signifiers," according to the Law of the Father (Mess Lethierry), for its signified: Déruchette. His arrival takes place in two chapters entitled "La Cloche du port" and "Encore la cloche du port." The name of the port is Saint-Sampson. Read: *(Toc-?) Sein-Sans-Son.* As Mess Lethierry rings the village bell-without-sound in celebration of the return of Durande, Gilliatt overhears a declaration of love between Déruchette and the pastor Ebenezer. Such is the bliss of the newly engaged lovers that they fail to hear the bell: "Ce tumulte, il est probable que le bonheur, ivre et céleste, ne l'entendit pas" (p. 769). At the very moment when the signified escapes from the signifier, when the law of castration is circumvented, a bell rings with uncanny silence in Saint-Sampson.

The novel concludes with Gilliatt's inhuman efforts to perpetuate that disjunction, to affirm that silence. As the ship bearing Déruchette and Ebenezer disappears on the horizon, as the rising tide engulfs Gilliatt, there remains, beyond subject and object, beyond author and novel, only the medium of infinite exchange, the sea.